C.J. MAH

Spiritual Disciplines

**FRONTIER PUBLISHING INTERNATIONAL
in association with
WORD PUBLISHING**

Word (UK) Ltd
Milton Keynes, England

WORD AUSTRALIA
Kilsyth, Victoria, Australia

WORD COMMUNICATIONS LTD
Vancouver, B.C., Canada

STRUIK CHRISTIAN BOOKS (PTY) LTD
Maitland, South Africa

CHRISTIAN MARKETING NEW ZEALAND LTD
Havelock North, New Zealand

JENSCO LTD
Hong Kong

JOINT DISTRIBUTORS SINGAPORE –
ALBY COMMERCIAL ENTERPRISES PTE LTD
and
CAMPUS CRUSADE

SALVATION BOOK CENTRE
Malaysia

SPIRITUAL DISCIPLINES

© C. J. Mahaney 1992

Published by Frontier Publishing International in association with Word Publishing.

All rights reserved. No part of this publication may be produced or transmitted in any form or by any means, electronic or mechanical, including photocopy, recording, or any information storage or retrieval system, without permission in writing from the publisher.

ISBN 0-85009-802-5 (Australia 1-86258-215-7)

Unless otherwise indicated, Scripture quotations are from the New International Version (NIV), © 1973, 1978, 1984 by International Bible Society.
Other Scripture quotations are from the New American Standard Bible (NASB), © 1960, 1962, 1963, 1968, 1971, 1972, 1973, 1975, 1977 the Lockman Foundation.

The quotations in the following studies are all used by permission.
Studies 1,4 from *The Practice of Godliness*, by Jerry Bridges, © 1983 by Jerry Bridges. NavPress, Colorado Springs, Colorado 80935, USA.
Studies 2,9,22 from *Ordering Your Private World*, by Gordon MacDonald, © 1985, Highland Books, Williams Building, Woodbridge Meadows, Guildford, Surrey. (USA/Canada Thomas Nelson Inc. Publishers, Nelson Place, Elm Hill Pike, Nashville, TN 37214, USA.)
Studies 3,7 from *Celebration of Discipline*, by Richard Foster, © 1978, Hodder & Stoughton Ltd., Mill Road, Dunton Green, Sevenoaks, Kent.
Study 6 from *Improving Your Serve*, by Charles R. Swindoll, © 1981, Hodder & Stoughton Ltd. (USA/Canada Winfried Bluth, D-5630, Remscheid, West Germany.)
Study 8 from *The Knowledge of the Holy*, by A. W. Tozer, © 1961, STL Productions, Kingstown Broadway, Carlisle.
Study 11 from *God Tells the Man Who Cares*, by A. W. Tozer, © 1980, STL Productions.
Study 12 from *Knowing Scripture*, by R.C. Sproul, © 1978, InterVarsity Press, P.O. Box 1400, Downers Grove, IL 60515.
Studies 13,19 from *Enjoying God's Grace*, by Terry Virgo, © 1989, Word Books, 9 Holdom Avenue, Bletchley, Milton Keynes, MK1 1QR.
Study 14 from *Know the Truth*, by Bruce Milne, © 1982 Inter-Varsity Press, 38 De Montfort Street, Leicester. (North America InterVarsity Press.)
Studies 15,20 from *The Disciplined Life*, by Richard Shelley Taylor © 1962, Bethany House Publishers, Minneapolis, Minnesota, USA.
Studies 16,27 from *Great Quotes and Illustrations*, compiled by George Sweeting, © 1985, Word Books.
Study 17 from *The Pursuit of Holiness*, by Jerry Bridges, © 1978, NavPress.
Studies 23,29 from *The Inner Life*, by Andrew Murray, copyright © 1980 by the Zondervan Corporation.
Study 26 from *The Power of Commitment*, by Jerry White, © Jerry White, published by the Navigators, Singapore, 1990.
Study 28 from *14,000 Quips & Quotes*, by E. C. McKenzie, © 1991, Baker Book House, Grand Rapids, Michigan.
Study 31 from *Prayer: Key to Revival*, by Paul Yonggi Cho, © 1984, Word Books.

Reproduced, printed and bound in Great Britain by BPCC Hazells Ltd., member of BPCC Ltd.

Making the most of the studies ...

Welcome to the Oasis study on *Spiritual Disciplines*! Many Christians want to be more disciplined but need some encouragement. Well, here it is!

We suggest that you take two days to cover each study and therefore two months to complete the book. You might want to work through the material more quickly, but if you take your time you are likely to benefit more. We recommend that you use the New International Version of the Bible (post-1983 version). The important thing is not that you finish fast, but that you hear from God *en route*! So aim to learn well and steadily build the teaching into your life.

Train for a crown

The apostle Paul said, 'Everyone who competes in the games goes into strict training. They do it to get a crown that will not last; but we do it to get a crown that will last for ever' (1 Cor. 9:25). 'We do it' — those are searching words for every believer. Many of us aren't training very hard and have become spiritually flabby.

With frequent reference to a favourite subject, sport, C. J. Mahaney takes us into the spiritual gym and helps us to tone up our spiritual muscles. He speaks as someone who is familiar with the struggles involved in mastering the various pieces of equipment — getting up in the morning, listening to God, prayer, giving ... He points out that success in public is dependent largely on private devotion and urges us to imitate the One who trained for and ran the perfect race.

The three sections under the main text relate to the teaching material. You may be asked to consider a particular discipline, to answer a question, or to do something practical. The questions have been designed to help you develop spiritual disciplines. Let the Scripture verses inspire you to throw off anything that hinders and finish the course.

Build a storehouse

The Bible says, 'Wise men store up knowledge' (Prov. 10:14), and Jesus underlines this when He calls us to '[bring] good things out of the good stored up in [our] heart' (Luke 6:45).

The 'Food for thought' section gives you the invaluable opportunity of hearing from God direct and of storing up what He says to you. **Please use a separate notebook** particularly for this section. Not only will it help you to crystallise your thoughts, but it will also be of tremendous reference value in the future.

As you study, refuse to let time pressurise you. Pray that God will speak to you personally and expect Him to do so. You may sometimes find that you're so enthralled by what He says to you that you're looking up many Scriptures which are not even suggested!

Finally, may God bless you through this book. May He help you to put aside past failures to discipline your life and draw you into a deeper relationship with Himself.

❏ STUDY 1

'The LORD does not look at the things man looks at. Man looks at the outward appearance, but the LORD looks at the heart'
(1 Sam. 16:7b).

It looks good

Do you ever feel that your knowledge about discipline is much greater than your experience of it? Maybe you can remember one worship meeting when God challenged you to sort yourself out. You were so keen to improve that when you got home, you made the mistake of publicising your new routine: 'daily Bible study and prayer at 5.00 a.m., and fasting every Monday'. Unfortunately, several Mondays later after awakening at 7.00 a.m. and not having had time to study the Bible, you were seen sitting in a burger bar sinking your teeth into a quarterpounder! You learnt then never to announce your intentions again.

I've got folders of notes that I've taken at meetings. When the preacher touched something that wasn't a part of my life, I used to write in a different colour ink, underline it or put asterisks in the margin. Now, when I read through them I think, 'Oh, I remember. That's the meeting when I dedicated myself afresh to God in that area.' Then I look at my present state and feel thoroughly convicted. It's far easier to start than it is to remain consistent.

In America, the television advertisements make exercise look and sound so attractive. The

▧ To confess

If we are honest, we have all made 'spiritual resolutions' which we have failed to keep, and these failures have made us feel guilty or convicted.

At the beginning of these studies why not wipe the slate clean? Confess your previous failures to the Lord and ask Him to help you as you work through these studies.

▧ To meditate on

Nothing is hidden from God.
'The heart is deceitful above all things and beyond cure. Who can understand it? I the LORD search the heart and examine the mind, to reward a man according to his conduct, according to what his deeds deserve.' (Jer. 17:9,10).
'He will bring to light what is hidden in darkness and will expose the motives of men's hearts' (1 Cor. 4:5b).

cameras pan round the gym and it looks as if everyone's thoroughly enjoying themselves. The men are muscular and the women are gorgeous. Nobody's sweating. They're smiling and are all wearing the latest designer outfits. You're inspired by them; you want to join in. But exercise isn't like that. It's hard work.

I've seen the film *Chariots of Fire* more than six times. It stirs you. You want to put on a new jogging outfit and run to the theme tune on your headset. But life isn't one big movie. As you move your legs your body begins to protest, 'Hey! What's happening?!' After a couple of days you have numerous muscle complaints and decide simply to adopt the 'jogging look'.

Many believers do that. We're inspired by great heroes of prayer, and try to discipline our lives. After about two days, our body is crying out for relief and we give up in favour of the 'spiritual look'. We deceive ourselves into thinking that learning about the Christian life is sufficient. It is not. God isn't interested in how many meetings we attend, books we read or tapes we hear. He wants to see the genuine article — people who submit to grace-motivated discipline and persevere, whatever it costs.

▓ Food for thought

➢ Read Matthew 21:28–32, the Parable of the Two Sons.

➢ Which of the two sons do you most resemble?

➢ Are you the one who is doing what his father wanted?

➢ Write down three specific things you know God wants of you.

_____

_____

_____

▓ To assess

Have you settled for looking good instead of disciplining yourself to be consistent in your walk with God?

Look through your old notes, etc. and make a list of things that God has challenged you about and you haven't followed through.

As we grow in the grace of self-control, we will experience the liberation of those who, under the guidance and grace of the Holy Spirit, are freed from the shackles of self-indulgence and are brought into the freedom of true spiritual discipline.
Jerry Bridges

STUDY 2

Then he said to them all: 'If anyone would come after me, he must deny himself and take up his cross daily and follow me' (Luke 9:23).

Secret preparation

You'll have to bear with me if I use a lot of 'sports' illustrations, I have a weakness for this particular subject!

Successful athletes inspire me. But I've noticed that the radio and TV announcers focus on the result, not on the hard work that led to the particular achievement. The stress tends to be on the athlete's gift, talent and ability, not on the rigorous training that was necessary. Certainly, gift, talent and ability play an important part in the success story. But if we concentrate on these things and on the resultant victory, we will overlook or minimise the amount of practice, discipline and sacrifice that went on before the event ever took place.

A friend and I were once given tickets for the college basketball finals at the University of Maryland. The tickets allowed us to go to the practice session the day before — something I was keen to do because the coach then was one of the greatest in college basketball history.

We stood on the side of the court watching our heroes do various drills which lasted for some two hours. The coach put them through different disciplines and permitted no one to impress the onlookers. There was nothing

▓ To do

Buy or borrow a sports magazine and read about the discipline that individual athletes go through to perform at peak level.

Let their stories inspire you to perform at peak spiritual capacity.

▓ To meditate on

Discipline yields eternal reward.
'Everyone who competes in the games goes into strict training. They do it to get a crown that will not last; but we do it to get a crown that will last for ever' (1 Cor. 9:25).
'No discipline seems pleasant at the time, but painful. Later on, however, it produces a harvest of righteousness and peace for those who have been trained by it' (Heb. 12:11).

exciting, no applause, no roar from the crowd. But the next day this team won the national championship. As far as I recall, the commentators didn't mention the training. But if you'd interviewed the coach or players, they'd have told you that their public success was due to what had gone on in private beforehand.

I've read articles by athletes who tell you about the sacrifices they've had to make in order to reach their goal. They talk about changing their eating habits, going to bed early, missing out on the activities that their friends are enjoying. They say how monotonous it is to repeat the same thing over and over, day after day, away from the applause of admiring spectators. Their comments are confirmed by other well-known people who have expertise in different areas. Great pianists, actors or writers will all tell you that to perform at peak level demands a private life of daily sacrifice.

It's no different in our relationship with God. The Christian life isn't purely a matter of gifting from the Spirit. It's about practice, discipline and sacrifice. If you want to know God intimately, to be sensitive to His voice, there's a price. Jesus modelled this for us. Will you?

▨ Food for thought

➢ Begin a study of Psalm 119.

➢ Write down, in a notebook, what practices, disciplines and sacrifices the psalmist makes in his walk with the Lord, e.g. practice — he meditates all day long.

➢ Think about practical ways in which you can begin to build these or other relevant disciplines into your life, e.g. hiding the Word in my heart — you could begin to memorise verses of Scripture.

▨ To assess

Write down what it will cost you to improve on your practice, discipline and sacrifice (be specific).

_____
_____
_____

Are you prepared to pay the price?

Are we going to order our inner worlds so that they will create influence on the outer world? Or will we neglect our private world and thus permit the outer sphere to shape us?
Gordon MacDonald

STUDY 3

Jesus' hidden life

Then Jesus was led by the Spirit into the desert to be tempted by the devil. After fasting for forty days and forty nights, he was hungry. The tempter came to him (Matt. 4:1–3a).

When we meet Jesus in the Bible, He's often exercising authority: teaching, confronting religious leaders, healing the sick, casting out demons or bringing words of knowledge or wisdom. The gospel writers saw His victory over sin, sickness and death, but they didn't imitate the modern-day announcers of athletic events. Rather than focus exclusively on Jesus' obvious public success, they exposed the reason for it — a private life of complete devotion to God.

If you ask a Christian what happened to Jesus in the wilderness, he will probably say, 'He triumphed over Satan on our behalf.' That's true. But it's not the whole story. All too easily we overlook Jesus' preparation for that encounter and forget the source of His strength.

Before Jesus met the devil He was 'led by the Spirit'. He was used to waiting on God. Deserts are not likely places to visit for any length of time, so Jesus must have been sensitive to His Father's voice to have headed in that particular direction. He was probably conscious too that He was going to meet Satan while He was there, so in preparation, He fasted for forty days and nights. There's the private practice, discipline and sacrifice! I love the understatement, 'he

▓ To consider

Our society is constantly looking for a quick fix, but in our walk with God, our strength, answers to problems, and power for ministry, etc. are directly proportional to our hidden life with Him.

Have you been looking merely for spiritual short-cuts?

▓ To meditate on

God's presence is enjoyable.
'You will fill me with joy in your presence, with eternal pleasures at your right hand' (Ps. 16:11b).
'How lovely is your dwelling-place, O LORD Almighty! My soul yearns, even faints, for the courts of the LORD; my heart and my flesh cry out for the living God ... Better is one day in your courts than a thousand elsewhere; I would rather be a doorkeeper in the house of my God' (Ps. 84:1,2,10a).

was hungry'! That's what was taking place away from the public eye.

Jesus made Himself vulnerable before this encounter because He knew that fasting would make Him spiritually strong. He gave Himself to it, and probably to the study of Deuteronomy from where His replies to Satan come.

Often we're more aware of the performance than the preparation. We long for success in our particular area of service, but want to avoid the sacrifice that may be necessary. When we face challenges, we don't experience victory because we haven't devoted ourselves to the means of grace privately. We haven't prepared.

The Twelve made the connection between Jesus' public power and His private devotion. That's why they didn't ask Him to teach them how to speak or perform miracles, but how to pray. Doubtless they often woke up to find that Jesus' bed was empty, and that when they found Him, He'd have been praying for hours. He wasn't trying to earn God's acceptance, nor was He trying to impress them. This was no legalistic activity; it was His delight. God wants our practice of the spiritual disciplines to be similar and our motive to be the same.

▨ Food for thought

➣ Over the next week or so read a biography of someone known for their prayer life, e.g. Praying Hyde, Rees Howells.

➣ In a notebook:

- make a note of any characteristics they displayed which you aspire to.
- write down anything else which particularly challenges you about their walk with God.

➣ Spend time talking to the Lord about changes you want to see in your own devotional life; ask Him to guide you and wait for His direction.

▨ To do

Do you consider fasting to be something for the spiritually mature or the high-fliers?

Why not miss one meal and spend the time praying? God's promise to you is if you draw near to Him He will draw near to you (James 4:8a).

Write down in a notebook what God says to you as you fast.

Fasting can bring breakthroughs in the spiritual realm that could never be had in any other way. It is a means of God's grace and blessing that should not be neglected any longer.
Richard Foster

❏ STUDY 4

Jesus listened

Crowds of people came to hear him and to be healed of their sicknesses. But Jesus often withdrew to lonely places and prayed (Luke 5:15b,6).

'The Son can do nothing by himself; he can do only what he sees his Father doing' (John 5:19b).

Isaiah prophesied about Jesus, 'The Sovereign LORD has given me an instructed tongue, to know the word that sustains the weary' (Isa. 50:4a). Clearly, the source of Jesus' encouraging words to the weary lay in His relationship with God. The verse continues, 'He wakens me morning by morning.' That's challenging. Every morning Jesus spent time with the Father. It was a consistent commitment. But what did God waken Him to do? Read on, '[He] wakens my ear to listen like one being taught.'

Jesus could easily have awakened to activity. He was a popular man. People were always pursuing Him. He was often surrounded by crowds who wanted to hear His teaching or be healed from their diseases. But He refused to be manipulated even by legitimate needs. He was not motivated by the personal desire to impress or achieve popularity. Instead, He was totally committed to His Father's will. And God wanted Him to wake up every morning, go to a quiet place and listen.

Jesus was intimate with God because He did just this. Morning by morning He found a place where He could worship, meditate, listen and

▓ To analyse

During this week make a note of how much time you spend alone with the Lord.

What proportion of that time was spent in listening?

▓ To meditate on

Prayer isn't just about speaking.
'The watchman opens the gate for him (the Shepherd), and the sheep listen to his voice. He calls his own sheep by name and leads them out. When he has brought out all his own, he goes on ahead of them, and his sheep follow him because they know his voice' (John 10:3,4).
'Therefore consider carefully how you listen' (Luke 8:18a).

talk to the Father. The relationship that He established with God through these disciplines gave Him the grace and strength to face three years of demanding ministry, hostility and eventual crucifixion. Even now the discipline continues since 'He always lives to intercede for [us]' (Heb. 7:25).

Jesus called His disciples to imitate His lifestyle, but He didn't motivate them by guilt. He didn't condemn them for sleeping in, or hammer them with a series of messages on prayerlessness. He simply let them watch Him. He provoked their curiosity and hunger for God. Then, when they asked Him to teach them to pray, He began to give them some specific instruction.

It's clear that the early church realised the vital importance of listening to God and this discipline was a major key to their success. Look through the book of Acts and you will see how often God intervened when people were waiting on Him. They'd learnt that if intimacy with God was a priority for Jesus, it had to be a priority for them too. So in the midst of a busy schedule, they found time to cultivate the ability to listen.

▓ Food for thought

➤ Read the following passages in Luke's gospel: 3:21–22; 5:15–16; 6:12–16; 9:18–21, 28–36; 11:1–11; 22:39–46.

➤ In a notebook write down instances when Jesus prayed. Especially note the time, the place, the regularity and the result or what happened next.

➤ If Jesus needed to do this what do you feel your response should be?

▓ To beware

You may feel that you need to make changes in order for you to listen more. Beware imposing externals on yourself such as 'I will spend half an hour a day listening.'

Jesus was intimate with God. Why don't you start by talking to Him and listening without any time commitment? Simply have a conversation with the Lord. As you spend time with Him, intimacy will grow and that in turn will motivate you to spend more time with Him.

One of the great privileges of a believer is to have fellowship with almighty God. We do this by listening to him speak to us from his word and by speaking to him through prayer.
Jerry Bridges

❏ STUDY 5

Those who obey his commands live in him, and he in them (1 John 3:24a).

If you listen

Hearing God's voice and responding to it — that's one of the greatest challenges that faces Christians today.

The theme of listening to God is emphasised again and again in the Scriptures. After the Israelites had come out of Egypt they celebrated the victory, then we read, 'There the LORD ... tested them. He said, "If you listen carefully to the voice of the LORD your God and do what is right in his eyes, if you pay attention to his commands and keep all his decrees, I will not bring on you any of the diseases I brought on the Egyptians, for I am the LORD, who heals you"' (Exod. 15:25b,26). God certainly promised that He would provide for His people. It's just that the provision came with a condition — listening that results in obedience.

Later God expanded on this. He commanded Moses to tell the people, 'You yourselves have seen what I did to Egypt, and how I carried you on eagles' wings and brought you to myself. Now if you obey me fully and keep my covenant, then out of all nations you will be my treasured possession. Although the whole earth is mine, you will be for me a kingdom of priests and a holy nation' (Exod. 19:4–6a).

▦ To ponder

Listening is different to hearing. Most of us can hear well, that is, we can 'perceive something with our ears'. However some of us do not listen well. Listening is active. It is not enough simply to hear something; we need to give focused attention to what is being said if we are to take it in and to respond. How good a listener are you? Ask someone close to you to give you their assessment.

▦ To meditate on

We listen in order to act.
'Hear, O earth: I am bringing disaster on this people, the fruit of their schemes, because they have not listened to my words and have rejected my law' (Jer. 6:19).
'Do not merely listen to the word, and so deceive yourselves. Do what it says' (James 1:22).

Notice the priorities in these verses as they apply to us today. First, God reconciles us to Himself and gives us a new relationship with Him. We rejoice in this, but salvation involves more than gratitude for the forgiveness of sins and the gift of eternal life. Secondly, it opens the door to obedience on a day-to-day basis. When we listen to God and do what He requires, He provides for us and fulfils His purposes through us. We become a unique people who individually and corporately manifest His character and power.

In the New Testament we are both exhorted to listen to God and expected to do so. On the one hand God commanded the disciples, 'Listen to him [Jesus]' (Mark 9:7), while on the other, Jesus declared, 'My sheep listen to my voice ... and they follow me' (John 10:27).

The idea behind Jesus' words is not that His disciples ought to listen and follow but that they do. As far as He is concerned, hearing God is not simply a requirement. It's a statement of fact, a distinguishing mark. Believers know God, listen to Him and obey everything He tells them to do. Let's live consistently with this truth.

▩ Food for thought

➢ Read James 1:23–25.

➢ Have you been deceiving yourself?

➢ Are you guilty of merely listening to the Word but not doing what it says?

➢ Go back to the list of things God has challenged you about but which you haven't followed up on (Study 1).

➢ Don't be condemned. Talk to the Lord about your list. Confess to Him that you have heard His Word but not acted upon it. Ask Him to go through your list with you and show you how to begin to do what He has told you to do.

▩ To confess

Are there specific areas of disobedience in your life?

What are they?

_____

_____

Ask the Lord to forgive you and ask Him to help you live a life of daily obedience.

The problem with most Christians is not that they don't obey but that they don't hear.
Derek Prince

☐ STUDY 6

As Jesus and his disciples were on their way, he came to a village where a woman named Martha opened her home to him. She had a sister called Mary, who sat at the Lord's feet listening to what he said
(Luke 10:38,39).

It's no time to listen!

To illustrate the importance of listening to God, I want to spend the next few studies looking at the story of Martha and Mary.

While Jesus and His disciples were on their way to Jerusalem, they stopped in Bethany where Martha opened her home to them. Now there's no indication that these thirteen men had actually been invited for dinner, so you can sympathise a little with Martha. Although she welcomed them without hesitation, she must have been somewhat overwhelmed. After all, she was running a home, not a restaurant!

What would be your initial response if thirteen church leaders suddenly turned up on your doorstep needing hospitality? Outwardly you'd probably be thinking, 'What a privilege!' But inwardly you'd be regretting the state of your home. Immediately they walked through the door you'd start apologising for the mess in the living room, and you'd be racking your brains for a way to feed everyone.

Thirteen individuals unexpectedly descended on Martha's home, and she must have been struggling. You couldn't find restaurants in that culture. You couldn't encourage your visitors to pop out for a burger. Martha had to prepare

▓ To assess

Do other things take a greater priority in your life than listening to Jesus (even good works)?

Mentally assess your priorities — where does listening to God come on your list?

Do you need to make adjustments? If so how will you start to do this?

▓ To meditate on

We must love God and others.
'Love the LORD your God with all your heart and with all your soul and with all your strength' (Deut. 6:5).
'Serve one another in love. The entire law is summed up in a single command: "Love your neighbour as yourself"' (Gal. 5:13b,14).

something, and she assumed that Mary would help her. But Mary sat and listened to Jesus.

It's one thing to cope with numerous unexpected visitors, but quite another not to have your sister help you. Martha was probably struggling. She was trying to please her guests, and she was probably projecting guilt onto Mary who was, in her eyes, being thoroughly insensitive and irresponsible.

Have you ever felt resentment towards someone who's taken advantage of you? You prepare a meal and when it's over, your guest simply leaves you to do all the clearing up. Or have you ever questioned the motive of someone who's tidying up for you? At first he's a superb servant, but as he continues to work, you catch certain accusing facial expressions, sighs and 'under the breath' comments. Then you wonder if his spirit is right.

Maybe Martha tried to get Mary to respond through eye contact and various 'humph' noises. After all, who gave Mary permission to relax when she should be serving? Was self-pity affecting Martha as she continued to prepare the meal for the group who had spontaneously arrived?

▓ Food for thought

➢ Look up Matthew 20:28 and Philippians 2:5–11. It is important to remember that serving is also a spiritual discipline and we should not overlook its significance. What is your attitude to serving?

➢ List any areas of service you are currently involved in.

_____

_____

_____

_____

➢ Is it important to you that you are noticed as you serve? YES/NO
What should our attitude be?

▓ To consider

Are there any times when we should serve and not simply listen?

_____

When are they?

_____

_____

If you are the type who needs a lot of strokes from people, who has to be appreciated before you can continue very long, you'd better forget about being a servant. More often than not, you will be overlooked, passed up, behind the scenes, and virtually unknown.
Charles Swindoll

❏ **STUDY 7**

But Martha was distracted by all the preparations that had to be made (Luke 10:40a).

A time to serve

When we look at Jesus' attitude to Martha, we might think that He was teaching against serving. This is not the case. The story is not releasing us to be lazy, selfish and irresponsible. God never calls us away from activity into an exclusive monastic existence of quietness and solitude. Indeed, the Bible is all about serving. So what's the main teaching point here?

It concerns the difference between service that's born out of a relationship and service that replaces a relationship. Martha was probably assuming that she had to prepare an unnecessarily elaborate meal for Jesus. She was putting it upon herself to overcater for His needs so it was her fault that she was overworked.

At this point I would like to redeem Martha's name because, after the death of Lazarus, she demonstrated remarkable faith. Then she said to Jesus, 'Lord, … if you had been here, my brother would not have died. But I know that even now God will give you whatever you ask' (John 11:21,22). She told Him that she knew that Lazarus would rise again at the resurrection and made this startling comment:

▓ To question

Do you assume you know what Jesus wants without listening to see if He really wants it?

▓ To meditate on

God speaks clearly.
'Do whatever he tells you' (John 2:5b).
'Wisdom calls aloud in the street, she raises her voice in the public squares; at the head of the noisy streets she cries out, in the gateways of the city she makes her speech' (Prov. 1:20,21).

'I believe that you are the Christ, the Son of God, who was to come into the world' (John 11:27b). These words came from a woman of outstanding faith and courage.

To return to the original story, Martha's error was this: she failed to take time, or rather make time, to listen to what Jesus really wanted. But she learned from her mistake.

Six days before the Passover a meal was given in Jesus' honour. But this time invitations were sent out and everyone who came was expected. Now we don't find Martha saying, 'I'm not serving this time. When Jesus arrives, I'll be sitting next to Mary and staying there!' We read, 'Martha served' (John 12:2b).

Martha wanted to make up for what had happened at that previous meal. The rebuke that Jesus had given her then didn't render her inactive, it changed her motive. She was a woman of initiative and obviously had a gift of serving. But her service had to be Spirit-born. It had to stem not from obligation but from a relationship with Jesus.

If you're not serving, you need to realise your responsibility to serve. If you're burning yourself out, you need to check your motive.

▩ Food for thought

➢ Read 1 Samuel 3: 1–10.

➢ Samuel heard the Lord but he didn't recognise His voice because he did not yet know Him. We know the Lord but would we recognise His voice?

➢ Write down how you personally recognise the Lord's voice.

▩ To reflect

Sometimes our serving can become a cover for not listening to God:

'I couldn't get into the meeting — I was sorting out a crisis in the coffee lounge/car park/crèche!'

Are you too busy 'serving' the Lord to hear Him?

True service comes from a relationship with the divine Other deep inside. We serve out of whispered promptings, divine urgings. Energy is expended but it is not the frantic energy of the flesh.
Richard Foster

❏ STUDY 8

He who did not spare his own Son, but gave him up for us all — how will he not also, along with him, graciously give us all things? (Rom. 8:32)

Don't you care?

When Martha saw Mary's irresponsible attitude, she reacted first against the Lord and then against her sister.

Maybe she was coming in with a tray of food when she stopped and abruptly interrupted Jesus' teaching session. 'Lord, don't you care ... ' (Luke 10:40b). It's incredible that she could attack Him in this way. But her rebuke was meant not for Jesus alone. The object of her frustration was Mary. So Martha's accusation was transferred to her. '... don't you care that my sister has left me to do the work by myself?' There's the self-pity. Then she dared to command God, 'Tell her ... (not "my sister" or "Mary") to help me!'

If Martha had realised that her comments were going to appear in Scripture, she might have restrained herself and feigned sincerity. But she was frustrated and probably felt that her outburst was justified, so she reacted. After all, she was the older sister and since Mary was enjoying the benefits of her home, she should take on some of the responsibilities too. Anyway, these thirteen men were the reason for Martha's busyness in the first place. Jesus should have known that. He should have been

▧ To consider

Are there any areas in your life where you are asking God 'don't you care'?

What are they?

_____

_____

Now talk to God honestly about how you feel. Ask Him to show you His perspective.

▧ To meditate on

God cares for you.
'The LORD is my shepherd, I shall not be in want. He makes me lie down in green pastures, he leads me beside quiet waters, he restores my soul. He guides me in paths of righteousness for his name's sake. Even though I walk through the valley of the shadow of death, I will fear no evil, for you are with me; your rod and your staff, they comfort me' (Ps. 23:1–4).

sensitive to Martha's situation and corrected this thoughtless woman at His feet.

'Don't you care?' she said to Jesus. I have to admit that on many occasions I've charged God like that. When I haven't waited on Him and listened, I've put a wrong interpretation on my circumstances and feelings. Then I've been tempted to challenge God that He doesn't care.

We can all relate to this — particularly in the area of unanswered prayer. A friend is praying in a similar way to you, but he gets a reply and you don't. Maybe you're single and want to be married, or you long to have a child. As the years go by, you see others marrying or having children when you're overlooked. Or you take someone to a meeting and he doesn't get saved, but your friend's relative does. While others are rejoicing, you're trying to rejoice with them, but inside you're crying, 'Lord, don't you care?'

These words must hurt God deeply, because no one cares more than He does. We must never allow ourselves to doubt His love for us. When we do, it's often because we've neglected to wait in His presence and listen to His voice. He wants us to turn every situation into an opportunity to trust Him. Let's do that.

▪ Food for thought

➤ Read James 3:1–12.

➤ Why is it important that we should control our tongues?

➤ According to James what is the mark of a perfect man?

➤ What is your response to this?

▪ To ponder

Sometimes we put our mouth into gear before our brain. We may lash out at someone when we are hurt, etc.

Look at Jesus' example . 'He was oppressed and afflicted, yet he did not open his mouth; he was led like a lamb to the slaughter, and as a sheep before her shearers is silent, so he did not open his mouth' (Isa. 53:7).

Ask the Lord to help you if you know that you are not in control of your tongue.

The love of God is one of the great realities of the universe, a pillar upon which the hope of the world rests. But it is a personal, intimate thing, too. God does not love populations, He loves people. He loves not masses, but men. He loves us all with a mighty love that has no beginning and can have no end.
A. W. Tozer

STUDY 9

And we know that in all things God works for the good of those who love him, who have been called according to his purpose (Rom. 8:28).

You're distracted

Martha was distracted by the things she needed to do. She was also 'worried and upset' (Luke 10:41b). People who don't cultivate the art of listening become easily distracted and lose a biblical or eternal perspective regarding their circumstances. Then they start worrying and becoming irritated. Worry effectively says to God, 'I don't think I can trust you.'

I struggle with worry — but never when I'm listening. When I'm waiting on God I have that inner assurance that He is sovereign over my circumstances, however perplexing they are. The Word is in my heart and I have an eternal perspective on what's going on. I know that God is using the difficulties to transform me into the image of His Son. Waiting brings peace and perspective. It releases us from anger and bitterness and delivers us from a hurried spirit.

Sadly, I do still find myself hurried and worried. I'll be in a hotel, hitting the elevator button again and again, as if my repeated action is going to make the lift come faster. Then I'll think to myself, 'C. J., what's going on? What kind of attitude is this?' Often, we're not even aware that we're worried and angry. It's the norm in our culture. Everyone flies round

▦ To question

Do you see something of yourself in Martha? Are you a worrier? Are you distracted?

Instead of letting your worries distract you from the Lord why not take them to Him, tell Him what concerns you and ask for His help.

Review God's faithfulness to you personally and allow trust in Him to rise within you.

▦ To meditate on

People who worry aren't trusting. 'Therefore I tell you, do not worry about your life, what you will eat; or about your body, what you will wear' (Luke 12:22b).

'The seed that fell among thorns stands for those who hear, but as they go on their way they are choked by life's worries, riches and pleasures, and they do not mature' (Luke 8:14).

at a frantic pace, trying to get everything done, unaware of their motive or attitude — like Martha. She exploded against Jesus for not caring and condemned her sister for being irresponsible. That's where worry and anger culminate — in criticism and comparison.

Do you know how it feels to be upset with people who refuse to be upset with you? No matter what you say, they remain calm. You struggle, become critical and start to develop a standard of comparison that's totally inaccurate and unbiblical. You're submitting to pride. You've taken on an attitude of superiority. Martha did that.

It's amazing that Jesus didn't interrupt her. He had every right to say, 'Do you have any idea who I am? How dare you command me! I created you.' But He refused to be provoked. Then, when she'd exhausted her frustration, He looked at her and said, 'Martha, Martha'. Whenever Jesus repeats your name it's serious. 'Martha, Martha, ... you are worried and upset about many things.' He didn't sympathise with her, and she didn't react against what He said. Maybe she realised that His words were true. Maybe they're true for you as well.

▨ To read

Distraction: to draw or direct one's attention to a different object or in different directions at the same time, to stir up or confuse with conflicting emotions or motives. *Webster's Dictionary*

▨ Food for thought

➢ Plan some time to be alone with the Lord when you can be free from distraction.

➢ Find a quiet place, make sure you will be undisturbed, do not look at your agenda/diary/to do list until after you have spent time with the Lord, pace yourself, relax in God's presence.

➢ You may find that you are still distracted by all sorts of things, but don't let them harass you. Begin to practise laying these cares aside and focusing your attention on the Lord.

➢ As you discipline yourself to concentrate on the Lord, you will be able to put aside what is not important and give yourself to what is.

If my private world is in order, it will be because, having faced up to what drives me, I listen quietly for the call of Christ.
Gordon MacDonald

❏ STUDY 10

Only one thing

'... but only one thing is needed. Mary has chosen what is better, and it will not be taken away from her'
(Luke 10:42).

'Here I am! I stand at the door and knock. If anyone hears my voice and opens the door, I will come in and eat with him, and he with me' (Rev. 3:20).

Are we involved in self-effort or obedience? Self-effort leads to burnout. We might be tempted to blame God or others for that, but ultimately it's our responsibility. We must make time for waiting and listening prior to activity.

Let's remember that it wasn't an effortless experience for Mary. She had to make a choice, and that involved discipline. Jesus invites us to discover more of Him, but He doesn't hammer on the door of our hearts. He just knocks. If you aren't listening, you won't hear Him. He's calling you to choose. He won't do it for you.

Our culture offers us various forms of fulfilment, but they're only temporary. Jesus said that what Mary was doing would never be taken away from her; it had eternal value. I don't believe that Martha's service at the next meal was taken away from her because by then it was born of the Spirit.

We must check that our actions are born of the Spirit. Are we being conformed to our society, becoming content with low-cost, convenient, comfortable Christianity? Some believers no longer use the words 'sin' and 'repentance'. Instead, they replace them with more attractive alternatives, adjusting the

▩ To consider

Are you someone who has tacked Jesus onto your life or have you given yourself whole-heartedly to Him?

You will only experience fullness of joy as you devote yourself to Jesus, cultivating an intimate relationship with Him.

Don't let this moment pass without making a response to the Lord. Give Him your devotion.

▩ To meditate on

God must be the focus of our life. 'One thing I ask of the LORD, this is what I seek: that I may dwell in the house of the LORD all the days of my life, to gaze upon the beauty of the LORD and to seek him in his temple' (Ps. 27:4). 'Seek first his kingdom and his righteousness' (Matt. 6:33a).

message to fit the culture. That's not biblical Christianity, it's marketing strategy, and it won't endure the test of eternity.

One day God will assess us. Our decisions have eternal consequences. Some of the things we do will be burned up. Others will bring us a reward which is beyond the temporary fulfilment that this culture has to offer.

God is challenging Christians to be radically different — not out of legalism, because we fear punishment, but because we love Him. Our culture tries to find its pleasure in partying. But fullness of joy is found in God's presence. He's looking for a church of Marys and Marthas, people who will not tack Him onto their lives but submit themselves to Him, listen to Him and obey Him with all their hearts.

We have a decision to make. Many voices will compete for our attention, tempting us away from the feet of Jesus. But we must be like the early believers, who devoted themselves to the spiritual disciplines and stood out from their society. God wants to fashion for Himself a people who are distinct, who challenge the culture, who don't just pursue their personal dreams, but serve His eternal purposes.

▓ Food for thought

➢ Read Psalm 42: 1–3.

➢ In a notebook write out, using your own words, your version of these verses, perhaps changing the picture of the deer to something more personally relevant to you.

➢ How does your desire for God compare with that in your version of these verses?

▓ To review

List all the church activities or forms of service you are involved in. Put a tick beside any of these which you know were initiated by the Lord.

With the rest, ask yourself:

- Is this activity self-effort?

- Should I be involved in this?

Take appropriate action to make any adjustments that are necessary.

Man is impressed by activity. God is impressed with obedience.
Terry Virgo

STUDY 11

'If anyone has ears to hear, let him hear' (Mark 4:23).

Are you listening?

Jesus said, 'Man does not live on bread alone, but on every word that comes from the mouth of God' (Matt. 4:4b). What physical food does for our bodies, the Word of God does for our hearts. If we aren't hearing God's voice on a regular basis, it's unlikely that we're truly alive in a biblical sense. But if we're healthy and hungry for God, we should be able to identify what He's saying to us. As we read the written Word, the Holy Spirit will reveal fresh truth to us and we will apply it to our lives.

God wants to speak to us on a daily basis, so every morning we should ask for guidance and expect His direction. However, this doesn't mean that we must consult Him about obvious things like where we should get tomorrow's groceries. I've met people who do that. They try to turn shopping into a supernatural experience and wait in their car until God gives them divine revelation! If they really listened, they'd hear Him saying, 'I've given you a brain, so please use it!'

Although we shouldn't approach God about relatively trivial issues, we should constantly be hearing His voice. This means that whenever someone says, 'What's God saying to you at the

▣ To do

Keep a diary of times you spend listening to God this week, and write down what He is saying to you.

▣ To meditate on

The Word is full of riches.
'The law of the LORD is perfect, reviving the soul. The statutes of the LORD are trustworthy, making wise the simple. The precepts of the LORD are right, giving joy to the heart. The commands of the LORD are radiant, giving light to the eyes. The fear of the LORD is pure, enduring for ever. The ordinances of the LORD are sure and altogether righteous. They are more precious than gold, than much pure gold' (Ps. 19:7–10a).

moment?' we can give an immediate and specific answer which is based on private or public encounters that we have had with Jesus. 'This is His current Word to me,' we will reply. 'And this is how I'm implementing the changes in my life.'

The issue is not 'Is God speaking?' but 'Am I listening?' God is always communicating through His creation, His Word and by His Spirit. But most of the time, it's a still, small voice which requires our full attention.

If we are constantly racing around neglecting to wait and listen, we shouldn't be surprised when we fail to hear God's voice. He won't be manipulated by our hectic schedules or co-operate with us if we haven't got our priorities right. Rather, He will wait until we decide to give unhurried, uninterrupted, quality time to Him.

Jesus said, 'When you pray, go into your room, close the door and pray to your Father' (Matt. 6:6a). God doesn't want you to be incredibly intense about hearing Him. You can't force Him to speak. But you can get on your own with Him and begin to cultivate the skill of listening.

▓ Food for thought

➢ Read Psalm 46:10. Being still is not simply a matter of being still physically.

➢ Make a comprehensive list, in a notebook, of ways in which you can be still, e.g. stop worrying, be quiet, etc.

➢ Consciously adopt these practices to help you as you spend time with the Lord.

▓ To assess

Are you still trying to squeeze God into your schedule, or is your schedule dictated by what He has been saying to you?

Think about how you allocate your time.

What criteria do you use?

I think it may be accepted as axiomatic that God is constantly trying to speak to men. He desires to communicate Himself, to impart holy ideas to those of His creatures capable of receiving them.
A. W. Tozer

STUDY 12

Listen to the truth

All Scripture is God-breathed and is useful for teaching, rebuking, correcting and training in righteousness, so that the man of God may be thoroughly equipped for every good work
(2 Tim. 3:16,17).

For the Word of God is living and active. Sharper than any double-edged sword, it penetrates even to dividing soul and spirit, joints and marrow; it judges the thoughts and attitudes of the heart (Heb. 4:12).

Among all spiritual disciplines, the study of the Word should always have the highest priority. Often we desire to read the Scriptures but don't know how. We lack not the motivation but the method. 'Where do I begin?' we question. 'How can I get the most out of this book?'

Well, for a start, how about making a few enquiries and buying or borrowing some books that will explain about Bible study? Why not get a study guide and go systematically through a particular book? Be sensible about it — don't start with Leviticus or Revelation! Try the Psalms or one of the gospels. And don't read the Scriptures as you might a novel. Before you start, ask the Holy Spirit to help you understand and expect God to speak to you.

When you work through a passage in a devotional way, ask questions of the text: What does it tell me about God? What does it teach me about life? How can I apply this to my life? When you get to this point, you can begin meditating on the truth. Then you can apply that truth to the tasks or pressures that lie ahead, and talk to the Lord about them.

Bible study is satisfying only when you allow God to speak to you personally through the

▓ To ponder

There is a vast difference between coming to the Scriptures with an attitude of faith, expecting God to talk to you, and simply coming to get your daily portion done.

What is your goal when you study the Word?
How important is it to you?
Does it take highest place among all the spiritual disciplines with you?

▓ To meditate on

God rewards seekers.
'You will seek me and find me when you seek me with all your heart' (Jer. 29:13).
'Ask and you will receive' (John 16:24b).
'He rewards those who earnestly seek him' (Heb. 11:6b).

Word. The overall goal is not to be able to say 'I've read this book in a year' but 'I know God more accurately and intimately.'

We praise God for the way that He is restoring the church, for tremendous times of worship, for prophecy and for greater obedience. But at the end of the day, it all comes down to one thing: an intimate personal relationship with God. That's why we were created. It's what God wants us to enjoy — not just in eternity, but now.

Jesus is waiting to give people fresh discoveries about Himself, but He won't do this for casual enquirers, people who are unwilling to seek Him diligently. He will reveal Himself to those who are earnestly seeking Him with all their heart, who are following the example He set by regularly devoting themselves to the spiritual disciplines.

The Lord is a jealous God. He longs to see you abandon things that draw your affections from Him because He knows that they will never satisfy you. He calls you to spend regular time in His presence. As you study His Word He will reveal Himself to you. As you continue in His Word, you will know the truth and the truth will set you free.

▓ Food for thought

➢ Using a concordance, look up references to 'the Word' and list in your notebook all the benefits that come to us through studying it, e.g. it is a lamp to our feet — it gives us direction.

▓ To consider

A big stumbling block to us when it comes to profitable study of the Word can be our past failure either to be consistent or to hear from the Lord through His Word.

Talk to the Lord about your past disappointments. Ask Him to help you as you begin again earnestly to seek Him.

I could say that the study of the Bible would probably be the most fulfilling and rewarding educational experience of your life. I could cite numerous reasons why you would benefit from a serious study of Scripture but ultimately the main reason why we should study the Bible is because it is our duty. He is our Sovereign, it is His Word and He commands that we study it.
R. C. Sproul

STUDY 13

In training

Your attitude should be the same as that of Christ Jesus: Who, being in very nature God, did not consider equality with God something to be grasped, but made himself nothing, taking the very nature of a servant, being made in human likeness. And being found in appearance as a man, he humbled himself and became obedient to death — even death on a cross! (Phil. 2:5–8)

If someone asked you, 'What's your goal in life?' How would you reply? Would you think 'I want to be successful' or 'I want to be rich' or 'I want to be happy'? Maybe you'd wonder what the right answer is from a biblical standpoint. One aspect of the answer is this: 'train yourself to be godly' (1 Tim. 4:7b). Godliness, not personal prosperity, is what we need to pursue. The Lord wants us to learn how to hear His voice with a view to our becoming more godly.

The church should be a company of people whose overwhelming motivation — both as individuals and corporately — is godliness, and who pursue it above everything else. They make decisions not on the basis of whether those decisions will give them success, wealth or happiness. Rather, behind every motive or action is the thought, 'Is this a godly aim?' While our ambitious generation tempts us to climb the ladder to prestige and power, God calls us to a different path and a distinct goal. It involves humility, servanthood and sacrifice and it leads to godliness and it is ultimately for the glory of God.

When Paul exhorted Timothy to 'train' himself, he used a word from which we get our

■ To pray

Is godliness your goal?

Ask the Lord to help you see His desire for you to be godly. Ask Him to reveal His love to you afresh and let your love for Him give you a new motivation to serve Him.

■ To meditate on

We should reflect God's character. 'What then? Shall we sin because we are not under law but under grace? By no means!' (Rom. 6:15)
'For physical training is of some value, but godliness has value for all things, holding promise for both the present life and the life to come' (1 Tim. 4:8).

word 'gymnasium'. So he likens our pursuit of godliness and intimacy with God to the athlete's devotion to private discipline in a gym. The results in both cases are reflected by the effort invested to achieve them.

We don't engage in spiritual disciplines to be accepted by God. Our acceptance by God and justification before God is based solely on the person and finished work of Jesus Christ. We haven't been called to originate or contribute to our justification before God. We cannot add to what Christ has accomplished. Justification is a gift we receive, not a position we achieve.

We might conclude, 'Well, if God loves us whether we obey Him or not, why don't we simply ignore Him and do what we want?' Because our justification through the blood of Christ is evidenced by a life of obedience. If Jesus is our Lord, people will see in us spiritual growth, maturity, change, godliness and discipline. Christians not only have a relationship with Jesus Christ, they are being conformed to His image as well. They are His disciples, His disciplined ones. Whatever He does, they also do. He is their example and they express their devotion by imitating Him.

▓ Food for thought

➢ Read through Romans 5,6 and 7.

➢ Write down your understanding of what the following mean:

- justification by faith
- the grace of God.

(You may find it helpful to use a commentary to do this.)

▓ To question

Do you feel you have to *do* things to earn God's favour? (If I do ... God will love me.)

Have you imposed laws on your own life? (I will do ... every day but if I don't God will punish me.)

We cannot do anything to make us deserve God's love. He has freely given us the gift of righteousness. Stop striving and enjoy God's love for you.

Godly discipline is not a work of legalism but of faith. The acid test is therefore: do I discipline myself because I've got to win God's favour or because I want to enjoy God's grace? The discipline of faith looks fully at what God says is already true and gladly lives in the light of it.
Terry Virgo

STUDY 14

Train yourself to be godly (1 Tim. 4:7b).

Train yourself

If Timothy had said to Paul, 'I'm asking God to train me to be godly,' Paul would have replied, 'Didn't you hear me the first time? I said, "Train yourself."' I've often asked God to train me. He just replies, 'C. J., I've made it very clear that you do that yourself by grace. Practise the spiritual disciplines every day and work at your relationship with me.' The result will be intimacy and godliness.

Some people seem to think that the Christian life is all about letting go and letting God. 'I just surrender myself to Him,' they say. Well, this may sound spiritual, but it isn't biblical. The Bible doesn't say to believers, 'Jesus will do everything for you.' We are exhorted, 'continue to work out your salvation ... for it is God who works in you' (Phil. 2:12b,13a). There's a dependent discipline involved here. We engage in spiritual disciplines dependent on His grace, while God brings about spiritual growth.

Maturity is not measured in years but in obedience. Someone who has been a Christian for three years may be more mature than someone who has been saved for ten. Three years' obedience and commitment to regular spiritual disciplines will make an individual

▓ To consider

In what ways can you begin to train yourself to be godly?

Why not begin to implement one of these ideas? Work at it and only when it has become a part of your life move on to the next.

▓ To meditate on

God strengthens us.
'I can do everything through him who gives me strength' (Phil. 4:13).
'"My grace is sufficient for you, for my power is made perfect in weakness." Therefore I will boast all the more gladly about my weaknesses, so that Christ's power may rest on me' (2 Cor. 12:9b).

more godly than someone who has trundled through ten years of low-cost, convenient Christianity. The important thing is not the passage of time but what we've done with it.

While I was at high school, we had an interesting six weeks of gym. The trampoline was the focus of our attention — not because we wanted to perfect our skills at it, but because we simply wanted to enjoy ourselves jumping as high as we possibly could.

Compare our casual attitude with the diligence exercised by the gymnasts in training for the Olympics. It's amazing what they can do. But what we see during the brief duration of the Olympics is the result of years of daily discipline in private. Our spiritual growth and progress will be no different. Personal growth and public triumph will be the product of daily practising the spiritual disciplines in private.

The responsibility for training can't be delegated to God. He's directed us to train ourselves. If our approach to training is casual and inconsistent, that will be reflected in a lack of growth. If our attitude is similar to an Olympic athlete, the result will be maturity. Which will it be for you?

▓ To encourage

List in your notebook any areas where you have been putting in hard work to train yourself, e.g. seeking to control your tongue.

Write down any improvements you have made.

_____

_____

Consider what would have happened if you had not put in any effort.

▓ Food for thought

➢ Read the Parable of the Talents (Matt. 25: 14–30).

➢ Which of the three men do you most resemble?

➢ What are you doing with what God has given you?

Nothing? ❏

A little? ❏

A lot? ❏

➢ Notice that the reward for diligence here is to share the master's happiness.

Scripture sets the need to be 'up and doing' in the work of sanctification, putting to death the old nature with its desires and putting on the new nature in Christ. Exhortations to holiness are never confined to vague appeals for surrender to the Lord or for entire submission to the direction of the Spirit; they spell out in detail the pattern of the holy life and urge us to make strenuous efforts to conform to it.
Bruce Milne

❏ STUDY 15

The sluggard craves and gets nothing, but the desires of the diligent are fully satisfied (Prov. 13:4).

It takes effort

Training in godliness doesn't come easily. Peter said, 'make every effort to add to your faith goodness' (2 Pet. 1:5b). To change involves the exertion of effort on our part.

I can't ever remember feeling like going to the gym for a work-out. I get there only because I've determined ahead of time that it's profitable. But as the hour approaches, my body always protests, 'C. J., don't overextend yourself. You worked-out only two days ago. You need to rest. How about tomorrow? Why not go only twice this week?'

The arguments don't stop when I've arrived either. They continue as I work out on each machine. 'Don't do this one today. What if your back gives out? Not the stairmaster! Oh, all right — but just do it at half-speed!' So there I am, sweating the minutes away alongside others who are doing the same. Later, when I put my coat on to leave, the only satisfaction I have is that I've finished!

Devotional times can be very rewarding; often they're just hard work. The problem is that we want something dramatic to happen every day, and anything less than an audible voice is a disappointment.

▨ To ponder

We live in a push-button age where everything comes easily to us. We are not used to working at anything because we do not have to. We do not even have to get to our feet to turn off the TV — we can use the remote control.

We need to remind ourselves that godliness comes through work. But it is worth pursuing. What is your attitude to hard work?

▨ To meditate on

We must obey regardless of feelings. 'Never be lacking in zeal, but keep your spiritual fervour, serving the Lord' (Rom. 12:11).

'Warn those who are idle, encourage the timid, help the weak, be patient with everyone. Make sure that nobody pays back wrong for wrong, but always try to be kind to each other and to everyone else ... Test everything. Hold on to the good. Avoid every kind of evil' (1 Thess. 5:14b,15,21,22).

I'm susceptible to this as I prepare to teach on a Sunday. I can spend over twenty hours working on a sermon. During the preparation I normally receive tremendous inspiration. But for the most part it's hard work: no open heavens, no visions, no angels gathered around my desk dropping words of knowledge into my heart. Occasionally it's even boring. At times I don't sense the presence of God either before or when I'm preaching. That doesn't disturb me; I understand the process and the effort involved. I depend not on what I feel but on the Holy Spirit whom I trust will work in the hearts of those who hear me.

It's the same with my devotional life. After I've prayed for a while I resist evaluating my emotional state to see how effective it's been.

God is transforming us into the image of His Son but this doesn't take place effortlessly. The only way is through discipline. Through daily dependence on God and devotion to the spiritual disciplines, regardless of our emotional state, we will eventually and inevitably experience intimacy with God and personal growth. Furthermore, our progress will be evident to all and the reason will be clear to us.

▓ Food for thought

➢ In a concordance look up all the references to the word 'sluggard' in the book of Proverbs.

➢ In your own words write in a notebook a description of a modern sluggard. How does this compare with you?

➢ Write down in a notebook any areas where you feel you could be making more effort.

▓ To assess

At times all of us make judgements according to how we feel. When we do so, we find it difficult to motivate ourselves in this whole area of spiritual discipline, because our emotions will not tell us how profitable it is, rather they will cry out for us to stop!

Ask the Lord to give you an understanding of how He is transforming you as you give yourself to the spiritual disciplines. Keep this before you when times of struggle come and keep focusing on what God has revealed to you.

A willingness to undertake the labor involved in becoming disciplined is the first step in achieving our desires
Richard Shelley Taylor

❑ STUDY 16

Knowledge

Make every effort to add to your faith goodness; and to goodness, knowledge; and to knowledge, self-control; and to self-control, perseverance; and to perseverance, godliness; and to godliness, brotherly kindness; and to brotherly kindness, love (2 Pet. 1:5b–7).

In addition to goodness, the apostle Peter exhorts us to add to our faith knowledge. Now knowledge is not number one on his list, but we are often inclined to make it number one on ours. We are impressed by someone who has qualifications, who is intelligent, articulate. 'Knowledge is synonymous with maturity,' we think. But that's not necessarily true because you can be intelligent and yet immature.

Often political candidates are elected on the basis of their skills as orators. 'If he has a degree and can communicate effectively, he must be the right man,' we assume. And we further assume that, 'What the country needs is more educated people.' Now I'm not against education, but what the country needs first is the fear of the Lord. This is an internal change in attitude of heart and the beginning of all true knowledge and wisdom.

When I was in my twenties, a friend and I went to a conference. We were particularly impressed by one of the speakers who was unquestionably the most knowledgeable man of the Word there, and the most effective teacher. Well, during one mealtime, my friend and I were sitting in a restaurant with this man and

▩ To consider

Ultimately the only knowledge that is important is our knowledge of God. More than that, it is not enough to know a lot *about* God, we need to know God Himself as a person, intimately. Is your relationship with God truly a relationship or is it merely head-knowledge about Him?

▩ To meditate on

We gain knowledge to become wiser. 'The fear of the Lord is the beginning of wisdom, and knowledge of the Holy One is understanding' (Prov. 9:10). 'Knowledge puffs up, but love builds up. The man who thinks he knows something does not yet know as he ought to know. But the man who loves God is known by God' (1 Cor. 8:1b–3). 'Where there is knowledge, it will pass away' (1 Cor. 13:8b).

his wife when they had a full-blown argument in front of us. Later, the couple gave us a lift in their car and the wife, who was obviously full of bitterness, turned to her husband and said, 'My husband, the great Bible teacher who doesn't do anything of what he teaches.'

My friend and I were sobered and went for a walk after that, purposing that we never wanted the same thing to be said of us. The man's knowledge didn't make us react against Bible study, but it revealed all too clearly that knowledge, apart from the fear of the Lord and proven character, is not the same as maturity.

To knowledge we must add self-control and perseverance. That eminent speaker may have had knowledge, but that was insufficient without self-control and perseverance. The early church were not only mentally informed by the apostles' teaching, they were devoted to it (Acts 2:42). By practising truth, their lives were changed.

Jesus' emphasis wasn't exclusively on our listening to teaching. He said, 'Now that you know these things, you will be blessed if you do them' (John 13:17). Do you want to be blessed? Apply what you know and you will be.

▓ Food for thought

➤ In a notebook draw a line down the centre of a page. On one side list what you know about God, on the other write down specific ways in which you have experienced this in your own life, e.g. God provides — testimony of how God has provided for you.

➤ Does your list reveal some areas where you have head-knowledge only?

➤ Read Paul's prayer in Ephesians 1:17–23 and make this your prayer for yourself.

▓ To assess

How are you consciously applying your knowledge of the Word?

_____

_____

_____

> We must observe that the knowledge of God which we are invited to cultivate is not that which, resting satisfied with empty speculation, only flutters in the brain, but a knowledge which will prove substantial and fruitful whenever it is duly perceived and rooted in the heart.
> *John Calvin*

STUDY 17

Be clear minded and self-controlled so that you can pray (1 Pet. 4:7b).

Self-control

Self-control has been defined as 'the ability to regulate conduct by principle and judgement rather than impulse, desire or outside pressure.' For the Christian, it's nothing to do with self-effort. Self-control is a fruit of the Spirit.

Some people interpret this to mean that all they need to do is sit back and wait for God to bring them into prayer. They quote Bible verses which seem to suggest that they have no responsibility. 'We're not into legalism,' they say. 'Grace frees us from striving.' True, but it doesn't free us from discipline. The Bible doesn't endorse passivity. It tells us that we have a redeemed will and that we must use it.

Self-control isn't effortlessly experienced — although sometimes we think it is. We go to a Christian meeting, have a powerful encounter with God and think, 'He's changed me! I'm totally different! I don't think I'll ever again have problems getting up early to study and pray! Shall I set my alarm? No, not after tonight. I'll be up before it goes off.'

But when morning comes, how many of you know that you're feeling a little differently from the night before? In no way can you justify lying

▩ To pray

Self-control is a fruit of the Holy Spirit in our lives. If you have been struggling to change through self-effort you have been relying on an ineffective resource. The Word of God encourages us to be continually filled with the Holy Spirit; as we do so the fruit of the Spirit will grow more and more in our lives.

Make it your daily prayer that the Lord will fill you with His Holy Spirit.

▩ To meditate on

Without self-control, we are vulnerable. 'Like a city whose walls are broken down is a man who lacks self-control' (Prov. 25:28).
'But the fruit of the Spirit is ... self-control' (Gal. 5:22a,23b).
'Be self-controlled and alert. Your enemy the devil prowls around like a roaring lion looking for someone to devour' (1 Pet. 5:8).

there between those warm sheets and say, 'Oh, Lord, just bring me out of this bed right now by the power of your Spirit. I want it to be of you, not me.' If all we are supposed to do is wait for God to raise us up, why does the Bible talk about the need for self-control?

Too easily we excuse our lack of discipline. 'Oh, I never could get up in the morning,' we joke. 'With my temperament I've never been consistent in study and prayer,' we rationalise. Such comments make the root problem sound so vague when it's actually so obvious. When God confronted me with my prayerlessness, He said, 'C. J., you're lazy.' That hit the mark, cut across all my excuses. I was allowing my emotions to rule my life.

Mature Christians have learnt to operate not from their feelings, which fluctuate according to circumstances, but from the ultimate authority of God's Word. They read that they must cultivate self-control and perseverance, so they actively seek to develop these qualities in their lives. They walk by the Spirit and find that self-control doesn't lead them into bondage but into freedom and fulfilment. Have you discovered that too?

▓ Food for thought

➢ Read through 2 Samuel 11—12:24.

➢ What were the results of David's lack of self-control?

➢ In what way does lack of self-control make us vulnerable?

▓ To consider

If the fruit of self-control is growing in our lives, what is our responsibility?

We need to exercise it.

Make a list of any areas where your self-control has been weak. Take just one area at a time and with the Holy Spirit's help begin to work at it. When you feel you are exercising self-control in this area, begin to work your way through the list.

Every Christian who makes progress in holiness is a person who has disciplined his life so that he spends regular time in the Bible. There simply is no other way.
Jerry Bridges

❑ STUDY 18

For the grace of God that brings salvation has appeared to all men. It teaches us to say 'No' to ungodliness and worldly passions, and to live self-controlled, upright and godly lives in this present age (Titus 2:11–12).

Training in obedience

The trouble with many of us is that when it comes to self-control we're stuck in unbelief. 'You don't know how often I've tried to be disciplined,' we say. My reply? 'I'm no different. I know what it's like to try and fail repeatedly.'

You decide to read through the Bible in a year, but by February you're stuck in Leviticus and falling behind by four chapters a day. In March, provoked by overwhelming guilt, you try to catch up by reading sixty-eight chapters in one sitting. A truly dynamic experience! This makes it more difficult the next time you consider daily Bible study. It's critical that you recognise this and do not submit to unbelief.

We are all training ourselves either in obedience or in disobedience. The training happens one choice at a time. If you're wise, you won't make long-term proclamations, like 'I need discipline in my eating habits, so I'm not going to eat another pudding for the rest of the year/my life.' You're setting yourself up for failure. Instead, just try to miss dessert today.

It's easy to train yourself in disobedience. You're out for lunch and after you've finished your main course, the waitress parks the dessert trolley right under your nose and a

▩ To do

Write down areas which need discipline in your life, e.g. TV viewing habits, daily exercise, reading, etc.

_____

_____

_____

▩ To meditate on

Discipline must be specific.
'The Spirit gives life; the flesh counts for nothing' (John 6:63a).
'Consider the members of your earthly body as dead to immorality, impurity, passion, evil desire, and greed, which amounts to idolatry ... But now you also, put them all aside: anger, wrath, malice, slander, and abusive speech from your mouth. Do not lie to one another' (Col. 3:5,8,9a NASB).

piece of chocolate cake sits there and says, 'I'm yours.' You gaze at it and start to rationalise your 'no pudding' decision. 'Well, I was a bit emotional this morning,' you think. 'I really must watch any tendency to legalism and extremism. After all, God gives us all things richly to enjoy. Wow! I've got a dynamic biblical reference for this activity!' And before you know it, you've consumed the cake and the Holy Spirit is saying, 'You've just made it more difficult for yourself the next time.'

How do you train yourself in obedience? You refuse the cake. It's the same with any habit. You depend on the Spirit and say 'no'. Then, as appropriate, you spend the time doing something more productive — like developing a spiritual discipline.

We're often stirred by preaching that calls us into a deeper relationship with God. We long for more of Him but are unprepared to change our habits and lifestyle to make it possible. If you really want greater intimacy with God, you must take dramatic action with regard to your overall lifestyle to make it happen. You must train yourself in obedience — one day at a time, one choice at a time.

▓ Food for thought

➤ Read Romans 1: 18–32.

➤ Here is the downward progression of mankind; they did not do what they knew to be right (glorifying God).

➤ When you do not do what is right in your own life, where does it lead?

➤ Write down in a notebook examples of people you know who have trained themselves in disobedience, perhaps in small ways at first. Where are they now?

▓ To resolve

Determine that you will train yourself in obedience.

Even today, say 'no' to whatever it is that ensnares you.

Gradually, as you learn to say 'no' more and more, you will notice that your habits have changed and you are becoming more like Jesus — one step at a time.

The general human failing is to know what is right and important but at the same time not to commit to the kind of life that will produce the action we know to be right and the condition we want to enjoy.
Dallas Willard

❑ STUDY 19

For Zion's sake I will not keep silent, for Jerusalem's sake I will not remain quiet, till her righteousness shines out like the dawn, her salvation like a blazing torch (Isa. 62:1).

Motive

As we have seen, trained bodies don't happen automatically! Your body and mind are in complete agreement that they don't want self-control. They refuse to cheer teaching about it and will rise up in protest if you start imposing any restrictions on them. Although in Christ you have a new nature, you still need to learn how to develop self-control by the power of God.

Firstly, you must have the right motive. Early in my Christian life I attended a conference with a friend. Now he was in the habit of getting up early to spend time alone with God. So when the alarm went off, he started dressing — and in order not to be outdone, so did I.

I remember sitting by a pond gazing round the campsite and envying the people who were still asleep in their warm beds. My eyes wouldn't focus on the Bible and I wasn't inspired to pray. I simply wanted my friend to know that I was in the habit of having daily devotions too.

Many of us are guilty of trying to project an image. We say things because we want people to be impressed with our spirituality. We 'let slip' that we prayed for two hours yesterday,

▓ To reflect

Think about the person you love most.

Spending time with them is not a duty but a delight. We love to be with them and to please them.

Is this how you feel about spending time with the Lord?

▓ To meditate on

If we're diligent, we won't be ashamed.
'I have posted watchmen on your walls, O Jerusalem; they will never be silent day or night. You who call on the LORD, give yourselves no rest, and give him no rest till he establishes Jerusalem and makes her the praise of the earth' (Isa. 62:6–7).
'You also must be ready, because the Son of Man will come at an hour when you do not expect him' (Luke 12:40).

that we fasted for three days last month or that we're planning to do something particularly sacrificial for someone during the week. Self-control must proceed not from pride, but from love. If we're attempting to discipline our lives in order to gain acceptance or approval, we will fail and be frustrated. God will never bless that motive.

The apostle Peter says, 'The end of all things is near' (1 Pet. 4:7a). Sadly, some people take this to mean that they can be passive and let the church slide gracefully downhill until Jesus returns. But Peter continues, 'Therefore be clear minded and self-controlled so that you can pray' (1 Pet. 4:7b). There's nothing passive or fatalistic about that. Jesus is coming, so we pray. And without self-control, we cannot be effective in prayer.

If we have a correct understanding of the end times, we will be motivated to pray. Jesus is returning for a glorious bride. Our love for Him and our desire to see His purpose fulfilled are proper motives to develop self-control for the purpose of prayer. Instead of trying to impress others we will be seeking intimacy with God and serving the church through prayer.

▓ Food for thought

➢ Read Matthew 25: 1–13, the Parable of the Ten Virgins.

➢ Compare the five foolish and the five wise virgins. How can we be ready for the return of the bridegroom? Why do we need to keep watch?

▓ To pray

Jesus is not coming back for a pathetic struggling church but one that is dynamic and glorious. That church will be made up of people just like you.

Be outward-looking: pray for the church, for your involvement in society, for God's kingdom to come, for your evangelistic endeavours. Pray that Zion's righteousness will shine out like the dawn.

Discipline is nothing to do with trying to impress God by outward Christian conduct. It is, instead, a natural response from our hearts to His love for us. We discipline ourselves not because we have got to, but because we want to. No one forces us to set the alarm clock. We do it voluntarily — because we look forward to spending time with Jesus.
Terry Virgo

❑ STUDY 20

How long will you lie there, you sluggard? When will you get up from your sleep? A little sleep, a little slumber, a little folding of the hands to rest — and poverty will come on you like a bandit and scarcity like an armed man (Prov. 6:9,10).

Goals

Some people are too accustomed to generalities. 'I must pray more,' they say, but fail to state exactly what this means. They have sluggard tendencies, and sluggards don't want to hear specific questions like, 'When ... ?' or 'How long ... ?' To these they reply, 'When the Lord directs,' and, 'In God's time.' They like to rationalise the Word of God and be mystically led by the Spirit. In reality they're lazy and will eventually be overtaken by poverty.

'The sluggard craves and gets nothing' (Prov. 13:4a). Most of us know what it's like to crave a fresh experience with God. We gaze enviously at some Christlike individual and covet his or her spiritual experience. Too easily we can be deceived into thinking that God is pleased with us simply because we're craving. But craving alone isn't enough. God is looking not so much for desire as obedience. We demonstrate that we've heard Him when we practise the truth.

The above verse continues, 'but the desires of the diligent are fully satisfied.' Diligent people set specific goals. Many of us make the mistake of trying to adopt other people's goals. We note that our spiritual hero consistently reads a veritable library of Christian literature and we

▨ To do

Ask the Lord to help you set some realistic targets for spiritual disciplines in your life.

Write down how you intend to start, even if it is only 15 minutes every day. After a week, review how you are doing. If you have not met your target maybe it was unrealistic for you and needs adjustment. If you have met your target you can begin to build on it.

▨ To meditate on

Wise people build for the future. 'But everyone who hears these words of mine and does not put them into practice is like a foolish man who built his house on sand' (Matt. 7:26).
'We do not want you to become lazy, but to imitate those who through faith and patience inherit what has been promised' (Heb. 6:12).

decide to follow suit. So we buy a pile of books and put them on our shelf. Three months later we haven't touched any of them, but we almost think that having them makes us more mature.

Then we learn that our hero spends two hours a day in prayer. We consider our five minutes a day and suddenly declare, 'OK, Lord, from now on put me down for two hours! And I'll study the Bible for an hour as well.' But God says, 'I'm not putting you down for anything. You're being totally unrealistic and you'll be overwhelmed before you start. Stop looking at others and start listening to me.'

People who don't jog are incapable suddenly of running a marathon. They build towards it. So if you've been making ridiculous promises to God, stop it! He's not requiring a marathon, just one step in developing the spiritual disciplines. Start small — with thirty minutes a day of prayer and Bible study — and be consistent. Seek God concerning where and how to begin and be specific. Learn from others without comparing yourself with them. If your plans don't have their origin in God, they will be a burden to you. If they're born of the Spirit, they will set you free.

▨ To question

Have you been deceiving yourself — thinking that desire by itself produces change?

Which of the suggestions in these studies have you actually put into practice?

▨ Food for thought

➢ Draw a horizontal line in your notebook. Mark the ends 'A' and 'C'.
If point 'A' represents where you were before beginning these studies and point 'C' represents where you would like to be — honestly assess the progress you feel you have made and mark a point 'B' where you feel you are now.

➢ You can frequently update this visual representation to help you assess your progress in the spiritual disciplines.

The world is full of naturally brilliant people who never rise above mediocrity because they will not make the sacrifice which superiority requires.
Richard Shelley Taylor

❏ STUDY 21

Action

For I have the desire to do what is good, but I cannot carry it out. For what I do is not the good I want to do; no, the evil I do not want to do — this I keep on doing (Rom. 7:18b,19).

Most of us are fairly happy to talk about discipline. But that doesn't change us. Discipline needs to be integrated into our lives.

The sluggard admits that he needs more discipline. But he always stalls for time. 'Ah yes,' he chuckles, 'I never have been able to organise my life. Maybe one day … ' He consistently refuses to acknowledge that he's actually disobeying God.

If there were a short cut to discipline I would have found it, because I've led the search. Discipline involves hard work and your body won't be comfortable with it. You see TV commercials for products that help you lose weight. The successful woman slimmer smiles and says, 'I lost three stone and I feel terrific.' It sounds easy but you know that losing weight isn't as much of a joy as the advertisers make out — neither is getting up in the morning.

Christians don't float effortlessly out of bed. I don't get a daily escort of angels calling to me, 'C. J., it's time to be with the Lord.' The alarm goes off; I silence it. I can hear the wind blowing outside and my body says, 'Don't move! We've found the perfect position. We're at one with the mattress. Don't be abrupt! Let's get into this

▩ To realise

Do you have trouble getting out of bed in the morning to pray?

You must face up to the fact that you are the answer to this problem. No one else is going to help you. You need to decide when you are going to get up, engage your will and do it. In this instance 'I can't' only becomes true when you let it. Resolve to be someone who says, 'I can and I will.'

▩ To meditate on

It's easier to give up than reap.
'Let us not become weary in doing good, for at the proper time we will reap a harvest if we do not give up' (Gal. 6:9).
'As obedient children, do not conform to the evil desires you had when you lived in ignorance' (1 Pet. 1:14).

gradually.' And I'm tempted to say, 'Lord I believe that we can be intimate right here!'

God has helped me overcome this. I get my left foot out of the bed and put it on the floor. Then I quote this verse: 'And if the Spirit of him who raised Jesus from the dead is living in you, he ... will also give life to your mortal bodies' (Rom. 8:11a). My right foot makes contact with the floor. Here's where I need the power of God because I can still sleep in this position! So I leap up and head for the bathroom.

I've met Christians who say, 'I don't have an alarm clock. I just let the Lord wake me up.' It's usually at 9.00 or 10.00. Paul said, 'I beat my body and make it my slave so that after I have preached to others, I myself will not be disqualified for the prize' (1 Cor. 9:27).

Someone commented, 'For some people, all that lies between them and fulfilling the call of God is a warm bed.' I'm not going to let a warm bed keep me from the call of God. I enjoy sleep, it's a gift from God. But I don't want it to be a hindrance to developing intimacy with God. I've often regretted too much sleep, but never regretted time in His presence at the beginning of the day.

▓ Food for thought

➢ Jesus was a man just like us. He, too, struggled with the same things we struggle with. (See Phil. 2:6–8; Heb. 5:8.)

➢ Read Hebrews 4: 14–16. How do these verses encourage you?

➢ 'Approach the throne of grace with confidence', talk to the Lord about those areas where you know that your flesh is weak. He is able to sympathise with our weakness and He lives to intercede for us.

▓ To do

Write down specific ways in which:

- the spirit is willing.

_____

_____

- the body is weak.

_____

_____

It's one thing to praise discipline, it's another thing to submit to it.
Richard Foster

❏ STUDY 22

Examine yourselves to see whether you are in the faith; test yourselves (2 Cor. 13:5a).

Guard your heart

Solomon wrote, 'Watch over your heart with all diligence, for from it flow the springs of life' (Prov. 4:23 NASB). We are diligent about the things that are important to us. Lack of diligence illustrates lack of concern.

If we are disciplined, we will often evaluate our spiritual health. That doesn't mean that we become introspective and sink into despair and condemnation. Christians don't wallow in feelings of worthlessness because God has declared them righteous in Christ (Rom. 5:18). So it's from this secure position that we examine our hearts. Evaluation will then lead to fresh motivation.

It's easy to assume that an increase in knowledge implies a healthy heart. This is not necessarily the case. The spiritual thermometer that tests our hearts lies in Jesus' words, 'Blessed are those who hunger and thirst for righteousness, for they will be filled' (Matt. 5:6). He's talking about people who are consumed with a desire for God.

Arthur Wallis said, 'If you're not hungry, you're not healthy.' The new birth creates hunger for God and opens our ears to His voice, but if we don't cultivate that desire, it gradually

▩ To analyse

What activities do you regularly give yourself to?

Are these innocent activities?

▩ To meditate on

It matters where your heart is.
'As water reflects a face, so a man's heart reflects the man' (Prov. 27:19).
'Since, then, you have been raised with Christ, set your hearts on things above, where Christ is seated at the right hand of God' (Col. 3:1).
'For where your treasure is, there your heart will be also' (Matt. 6:21).

subsides. We become dull of hearing and our lives are no longer characterised by the same zeal that we once had. We may be familiar with biblical principles, but we are no longer passionate for God Himself.

An absence of physical appetite usually means that you're unhealthy. If your spiritual appetite has subsided, there's a disease present and it's imperative that you consult God about it. You must take whatever medicine He prescribes, no matter how drastic it is.

For the majority of us, the illness isn't ongoing rebellion, it's innocent activities which are not sinful in themselves but which have become distracting and addictive. Whatever we constantly focus our attention on forms our desire. So if we are giving ourselves to an activity, our desire will form in that direction.

We must deal radically with any innocent activity that preoccupies us and hinders our sensitivity to God. What are these activities? In the next few studies I'd like to give you some examples. And I'd also like to challenge you to be honest with yourself, to examine your heart and see what adjustments you need to make to restore your hunger for God.

■ Food for thought

➢ In a notebook make a list of the characteristics of both spiritual health and sickness.

➢ Talk to the Lord about your spiritual health. Tell Him what your desires are. Ask Him to help you with fresh motivation.

■ To challenge

Examine your heart. Ask yourself:

- Am I hungry for God?
- Am I dull of hearing?
- Is my life characterised by the same zeal I once had?

The development and maintenance of our inner worlds should be our highest priority. We must choose to keep the heart. Its health and productivity cannot be assumed, it must be constantly protected and maintained.
Gordon MacDonald

STUDY 23

In vain you rise early and stay up late, toiling for food to eat (Ps. 127:2a).

Time for bed

A few years ago my wife and I were talking to a couple who told us that they got up to pray at 5.00 every day. I immediately joked that I had a problem getting up in the morning. The husband smiled, looked at me and said gently, 'Your problem isn't getting up in the morning. It's going to bed at night.' His words pierced my heart.

My wife had been trying to tell me this for a long time — particularly concerning meetings in our home. She'd ask me why we had to talk about sport for two hours and then begin counselling and ministry at 10.00! I'd say that we couldn't get to bed any earlier because at 10.00 the power of God was present. She'd then say that she personally felt that God could move at 8.00 and that we could be in bed by 10.30. With a little more leadership on my part I took notice.

I liked to say I was a night person, that I came alive after 10.00. When I got home after a busy day I'd assume that I had a right to the sports page, some chocolate and a glass of milk. 'I need this,' I thought. 'I deserve this. It's my time to relax.' So I'd read until midnight or later, then I'd go to bed and set the alarm for

▓ To question

What time do you normally go to bed?

What determines when you go to bed?

- tiredness
- TV programmes
- desire to get up early
- social life
- other (specify)

▓ To meditate on

We must learn when to sleep.
'Laziness brings on deep sleep' (Prov. 19:15a).
'Do not love sleep or you will grow poor; stay awake and you will have food to spare' (Prov. 20:13).
'Could you men not keep watch with me for one hour? ... Watch and pray so that you will not fall into temptation. The spirit is willing, but the body is weak' (Matt. 26:40b,41).

5.30. When it rang, I'd automatically silence it and fall asleep again. Then I'd go into my day without the internal resources to handle what was going on.

Someone once prophesied in a meeting, 'You're part of a modern generation who stubbornly refuse to crucify their night life.' That's so true, and it often seems unavoidable.

Housegroup leaders feel obliged to stay up. They start the ministry too late or allow the meeting to go on too long because they don't want to hurt people's feelings. This can stop. There will always be people who try to hang on after the meeting is over. They need to become sensitive to their leaders and the leaders must learn to speak the truth in love.

When God's arrow pierced my heart I started making changes. Now I'm normally in bed by 11.00 and up between 5.30 and 6.00. This is not meant to be the pattern for everyone. It's just that I can teach about spiritual disciplines and find that people can't engage in them because they're not getting to bed early enough.

I've found the most effective undistracting time to be the morning. Do you need to crucify your night life?

▨ Food for thought

➢ Compare the following verses from the Psalms: 5:3, 55:17, 59:16, 88:13, 90:14, 92:2, 143:8.

➢ In what spiritual disciplines does the psalmist engage in the mornings? It is not important when we spend time with the Lord but it is important that it is regular and consistent. Most people do find the mornings the best time for this. If however that is not the case for you, make sure that you do spend some other regular time alone with the Lord. It is so easy to deceive ourselves into believing that we are spending regular times in prayer, etc. even when we are not.

▨ To challenge

Are you serious about establishing a consistent discipline of time alone with the Lord?

Are you prepared to sacrifice evening entertainment for morning intimacy with God?

Next to receiving Christ as Saviour, and claiming the Baptism of the Holy Spirit, we know of no act attended with larger good to ourselves or others, than the formation of an indiscourageable resolution to keep the morning watch, and spend the first half hour of the day alone with the Lord.
Mr Mott

STUDY 24

Be very careful, then, how you live — not as unwise but as wise, making the most of every opportunity, because the days are evil (Eph. 5:15,16).

Television

The television has been described as one of the greatest thieves of our time. When the faculty of a college invited an interior decorator to plan the furniture arrangement of the student lounge, he said, 'If you put the TV set in the centre of the room you can forget about study sections, games or conversation.' The same principle applies in the home. If the television dominates our lives, it will rob us of fellowship with God and with one another.

God calls us to be holy. The cultivation of holiness takes time, and time can be used only once. There are, indeed, some very helpful and educational programmes on the television, but if we become slaves to it, we will squander a large percentage of our time on trivia. We must monitor our viewing habits. We must be masters of our time.

The TV industry knows that 'prime time' viewing is during the evening and at weekends. That's also the prime time for Christians to engage in spiritual activities or to build relationships. I read about one leader who was considering the place of the television in his home. He discovered that exciting serials often began on Sundays and realised that they

■ To do

Make a note of how many hours of television you watch this week. At the end of the week ask yourself:

- Do you need to do something about it?
- Ask God to help you set some goals, i.e. one hour less a week.

Remember any time you save should be used profitably.

■ To meditate on

Prime time must be reserved for God. 'There is a time for everything, and a season for every activity under heaven' (Eccl. 3:1).
'Do not love the world or anything in the world ... The world and its desires pass away, but the man who does the will of God lives for ever' (1 John 2:15a,17).

conflicted with the best opportunities for the family to talk, plan and pray together. He had a choice: TV or family. Family came out on top.

Parents, are you aware of your children's viewing habits? Do you know when and what they're watching? For years Carolyn and I restricted our children to a maximum of half an hour's TV every day (with periodic exceptions), and instilled into them a love of reading. I regularly take them to the Christian bookshop and they know that I am always ready to give them money for books.

Relationships do not develop when everyone sits glued to the television. If this is happening in your home you must do something radical about it. Now this doesn't mean that you become legalistic. If you call on a friend who happens to be watching an afternoon show, you don't project guilt and come across as self-righteous and superior. You identify your own priorities and work out for yourself what place the television should play in your life. You may even decide to get rid of it altogether.

Let's stop idling away the hours. God is looking for disciplined people who invest their prime time in the pursuit of holiness.

▩ Food for thought

➢ As you watch any TV programmes this week, keep a notebook beside you and write down any ungodly attitudes, morals, etc. which are portrayed.

➢ Is the entertainment value of these programmes more important to you than what you are feeding on from them?

▩ To identify

Why do you watch TV?

What else could you spend the time doing?

How could you change your viewing habits? Identify some steps you could take.

> I'm learning that people can hate a lot of television, hate their own viewing habits, hate what it does to them and their families and still think it's bizarre that anyone wants to get rid of it.
> *Jerry Mander*

❏ STUDY 25

Films and Videos

Whatever you do, do it all for the glory of God (1 Cor. 10:31b).

Nothing is to be rejected if it is received with thanksgiving (1 Tim. 4:4b).

Let the peace of Christ rule in your hearts (Col. 3:15a).

A few years ago several mainline denominations commissioned a major survey which investigated the media habits of American Christians. A questionnaire was handed out which asked believers to list the last five films that they had seen. The results were shocking. Those conducting the survey concluded that the viewing habits of believers were no different from unbelievers — except that the believers added a few religious programmes to their diet.

I am disturbed by the lack of discernment among many Christians today. Often they don't study the content of a film at all. Instead, they trust those who set the ratings, those who are not judging according to biblical standards. This is unwise. We must never rely on the world's evaluation of what is appropriate and what is not. Rather, we must assess films and videos from a biblical perspective.

Paul gives us clear guidelines regarding how to evaluate things which are not specifically mentioned in Scripture:
1. Can I do this to the glory of God?
2. Can I thank Him for it?
3. Does it violate Philippians 4:8?

▓ To ask

What was the last film/video you watched?

How would it rate if you applied the three tests given here?

Why did you choose to see it?

▓ To meditate on

Transformation is by mind-renewal. 'Do not conform any longer to the pattern of this world, but be transformed by the renewing of your mind. Then you will be able to test and approve what God's will is — his good, pleasing and perfect will' (Rom. 12:2). 'Whatever is true, ... noble, ... right, ... pure, ... lovely, ... admirable — if anything is excellent or praiseworthy — think about such things' (Phil. 4:8).

You need to apply these tests whenever you're thinking of going to the cinema or planning to hire a video. Whenever possible, study the reviews prior to attending a film or obtaining a video. Normally these will provide the information necessary for you to make a wise decision.

Some believers have protested to me, 'If that's the criterion, I'm not likely to see any films or videos at all! And I really don't think that's fair.' But are we justified in saying, 'I have a right to these things; I demand satisfaction'? People may say to me, 'You're a legalist.' But that's not so. I'm simply trying to pursue holiness and avoid temptation wherever I can.

Continuous film-watching is the mark of an empty, bored generation. When appropriate we should enjoy a film or video, but let's be wise and discerning.

Let's also recognise that the more we watch unhelpful films, the more we will become desensitised to sin and that will affect our passion for God as well. Let's develop and maintain our convictions from God's Word and set an example for others to follow.

▓ Food for thought

➢ Re-read Romans 1:18—2:16.

➢ How does the ungodliness in this passage compare with the lifestyles portrayed in films you have watched?

➢ How does God view such people?

➢ What should our attitude be?

▓ To do

Work out your own viewing criteria and list them below.

_____

_____

_____

With all this degeneracy in current movies one would expect that most Christians would be greatly offended by it and refuse to go. Tragically this is not the case. Christians have been seduced into accepting degenerate movie content and many have simply lost a sensitivity to vulgarity, sexual explicitness, brutal violence and ungodly lifestyles in the movies.
Dr Evans

❏ STUDY 26

Hobbies/Career

For physical training is of some value, but godliness has value for all things, holding promise for both the present life and the life to come (1 Tim. 4:8).

In his book, *The Power of Commitment*, Jerry White says, 'One of the significant measures of a person's spiritual commitment is what he does with his discretionary or leisure time.'

A primary goal of our culture is relaxation. People almost demand the right to have time in which to pursue their hobbies and sports. Christians too need to relax and be refreshed. That's why it's important for us to make the most of the leisure time that God has given us.

But we must be careful. I've talked to Christians who appear more passionate about their hobbies and sports than about Jesus and the church. 'I can't find the time for consistent Bible study and prayer,' they say. But they seem to make time for their leisure activities. When we begin to idolise recreation, God will intervene — not to spoil our fun but to remind us that the ultimate pleasure comes from being in His presence, hearing His voice and doing His will. We must get our priorities right.

We must also watch our careers. People everywhere are striving to make something of their lives: going for the highest qualifications, seeking the best positions. The world is selfishly preoccupied. It cares little for others.

▧ To consider

List in a notebook the pursuits you give most time to.

Do you give more time to your leisure pursuits or career than to cultivating your relationship with the Lord?

Decide now where your priorities should be and begin to adjust your commitments accordingly.

▧ To meditate on

God has a plan for you.
'For we are God's workmanship, created in Christ Jesus to do good works, which God prepared in advance for us to do' (Eph. 2:10).
'Let us run with perseverance the race marked out for us' (Heb. 12:1b).

Some Christians have allowed their careers to eclipse their passion for Jesus. They no longer hear God, their family relationships are strained, and although they still attend worship meetings, their zeal for the Lord has waned.

Compare these believers with others who have actually turned down opportunities to further their careers. Tom, a psychiatrist, completed his medical training with a three-year psychiatric residency. Initially he was so wrapped up in his own pursuits that he had no time for the church. But in the third year, God challenged him and changed his heart.

'Career is not primary,' he says. 'My priority is the church, the people we are sharing our lives with, the people that we love.' His wife, who works in the office in his clinic, says that they regularly receive offers of more lucrative positions. But they just throw them away.

The world will accept promotion just because it's offered. Christians must not be so hasty. Does Jesus want you to take it? Will you become too busy for Him or His people? What's your motivation — God or mammon? Any decision which hinders your spiritual development is not from God.

▧ To ascertain

Look up the definition of the word 'commitment' in a dictionary. Write down in your own words what it means to be committed to the Lord and His church.

_____

_____

_____

▧ Food for thought

➢ Read Acts 2:42–47.

➢ Absorb the flavour of New Testament church life. Imagine what changes would have to be made in your church if this kind of commitment were to be expressed.

➢ Write down how you personally can devote yourself:

- to the apostles' teaching
- to fellowship
- to the breaking of bread
- to prayer.

➢ What effect will this have on your leisure time? Are you prepared to pay this price?

Some Christians don't feel the need to commit themselves to any local body of believers. They see themselves simply as members of the body of Christ at large and do not give their allegiance to any local assembly, thereby totally failing to grasp the fundamental purpose of body life as expressed in the New Testament.
Terry Virgo
New Frontiers Magazine, May 1989

❏ STUDY 27

The M Word: Money

The ground of a certain rich man produced a good crop ... he said, ' ... I will tear down my barns and build bigger ones, and there I will store all my grain and my goods. And I'll say to myself, "You have plenty of good things laid up for many years. Take life easy; eat, drink and be merry"'
(Luke 12:16b,18–19).

Many rich people threw in large amounts. But a poor widow came and put in two very small copper coins, worth only a fraction of a penny ... Jesus said, ' ... They all gave out of their wealth; but she, out of her poverty, put in everything — all she had to live on'
(Mark 12:41b–42, 44).

The issue of finance is at the heart of discipleship. There's a direct relationship between your spiritual condition and your attitude towards money and possessions. The way you use your money reveals where your commitment lies and what you value.

Jesus said, 'If your eyes are good, your whole body will be full of light. But if your eyes are bad, your whole body will be full of darkness' (Matt. 6:22b,23a). The context of these verses concerns an understanding of economics which is radically different from that of our culture. We see clearly when we have decided that God, not money, is our master (Matt. 6:24).

The rich man of Luke 12:16–21 had bad eyesight. Our society would honour someone like this. He was planning for a cosy future but God called him a fool! He wasn't stupid because he was rich. His problems were independence and pride. 'I', 'my' he repeated. He lived denying the brevity of life and the certainty of death. He was a fool.

The poor widow of Mark 12:41–44 had good eyesight. Her values and commitment were undeniably clear and my life changes every time I get near her. I imagine meeting her

▪ To consider

Are you a regular giver to the work of the church?

Do you give to the poor?

What proportion of your income do you give to the Lord?

Is your giving in line with what Scripture teaches?

▪ To meditate on

God blesses givers.
'Give, and it will be given to you. A good measure, pressed down, shaken together and running over, will be poured into your lap. For with the measure you use, it will be measured to you' (Luke 6:38).
'Sell your possessions and give to the poor. Provide purses for yourselves that will not wear out, a treasure in heaven that will not be exhausted'
(Luke 12:33a).

outside the temple. 'I've just put two coins in the treasury,' she says. 'They were all I had to live on.' Do I think, 'What an irresponsible decision!' or, 'What an outstanding act of faith!'? Jesus commended her as an example for us all.

The material world isn't evil. God wants us to enjoy His gifts (1 Tim. 6:17b). But materialism is probably our most subtle opponent in the West. It distorts our eyesight, encourages covetousness and tempts us to pursue prosperity, not godliness. I'm provoked that one day I will have to give account to Almighty God for what I have done with His resources.

How's your eyesight? Do you admire the rich fool or the poor widow? Which one are you emulating? If your eye is sound, you will follow the widow's example and will invest your finances in God's purposes. People won't understand it. But you must see what they can't. Your motivation must not be the same as theirs. Where you invest your finances is a definitive statement concerning whether your values are eternal or temporal. Is it possible you need an eye examination from a biblical perspective?

▓ Food for thought

➣ Read Matthew 6:24.

➣ In a notebook write down how we can serve God and how we serve money.

➣ Why can't we serve both God and money? Which are you serving?

▓ To challenge

God's promise to us is that if we give to Him He will provide for our needs. In Malachi 3:10 He even suggests that we test Him in this.

If your personal finances are not in order, the first step you should take is to begin to give regularly to the Lord; He will then meet your needs as He has promised.

How we use our money demonstrates the reality of our love for God. In some ways it proves our love more conclusively than depth of knowledge, length of prayers or prominence of service. These things can be feigned, but the use of our possessions shows us up for what we actually are.
Charles Caldwell Ryrie

❏ **STUDY 28**

Treasures in heaven

Will a man rob God? Yet you rob me ... You are under a curse — the whole nation of you — because you are robbing me. Bring the whole tithe into the storehouse, that there may be food in my house. Test me in this ... and see if I will not throw open the floodgates of heaven and pour out so much blessing that you will not have room enough for it (Mal. 3:8–10).

Whoever sows sparingly will also reap sparingly, and whoever sows generously will also reap generously (2 Cor. 9:6).

How do we store up for ourselves treasures in heaven? We begin by tithing to the storehouse, the local church. According to God, if we're not doing this, we're stealing from Him and restricting His provision in our lives. In response to our tithing He promises to open the floodgates of heaven and pour a blessing on us.

But it doesn't stop at tithes, it goes on to offerings. The Macedonians, out of their 'extreme poverty' gave 'even beyond their ability' (2 Cor. 8:2b,3b) — as did the poor widow. We may think, 'It's a difficult time' but God still challenges us to 'excel in this grace of giving' (2 Cor. 8:7b) and provokes us to stop pouring money into unnecessary incidentals.

Sometimes people long to relate wonderful testimonies of God's provision. They fail to realise that abundance comes not by wishing but by sowing. You want to reap generously? You must first sow generously.

'Each man should give,' says Paul (2 Cor. 9:7a). There's no question. If you're a Christian, you are giving — not what you feel compelled by others to give, but what you have decided in your own heart because 'God loves a cheerful giver' (2 Cor. 9:7b). This doesn't mean, 'If you're

▒ To question

Are you a good steward of the money the Lord has given you?

Make a list of any items you have purchased in the last month which cost £10 or more.

Could you have done without any of these items?

What else could you have done with the money?

▒ To meditate on

God notices how we give.
'Woe to you Pharisees, because you give God a tenth of your mint, rue and all other kinds of garden herbs, but you neglect justice and the love of God. You should have practised the latter without leaving the former undone' (Luke 11:42).
'It is more blessed to give than to receive' (Acts 20:35b).

not cheerful, don't give.' If you're not cheerful you can still be obedient. As you are obedient you'll become cheerful.

God promises to 'supply and increase our store of seed' (2 Cor. 9:10b). Too many of us are consumer Christians. God blesses us with seed to invest but we accumulate possessions. We gain a promotion or receive a windfall and assume that we can now afford things. But that's not Kingdom economics. God says, 'I'm prospering you, not so that you can accumulate, but so that you can invest.' In other words, not to raise our standard of living but to raise our standard of giving.

So when God prospers us we don't sell everything since 'God ... richly provides us with everything for our enjoyment' (1 Tim. 6:17-19). As long as we know God has provided it, we can enjoy it. But we are commanded, not asked, to be generous.

Giving will bring personal reward, but our primary motive is the spread of the gospel and the glory of God. Do you want to establish His Kingdom throughout the earth? Then it makes sense to invest your treasure where you'll get the best interest and return, doesn't it?

▓ Food for thought

➢ Find out what your church is doing to support world mission.

➢ Investigate ways in which you personally could become more involved.

➢ Write to various Christian agencies, find out what work they are involved in and how you can support them.

➢ Ask the Lord whether you should be committed to giving to this work.

➢ Your gift may for example pay for Bibles for Eastern block or third world countries.

▓ To reflect

Are you aware of the financial needs of those around you?

Is there someone you could help immediately by giving them a gift of money, food parcel or similar?

Money may be used as a universal passport to everywhere except heaven and as a universal provider for everything except happiness.

STUDY 29

Let us purify ourselves from everything that contaminates body and spirit, perfecting holiness out of reverence for God (2 Cor. 7:1b).

And we ... are being transformed into his likeness with ever-increasing glory, which comes from the Lord, who is the Spirit (2 Cor 3:18).

Be transformed

One of the greatest problems in Christendom is this: we don't understand that we're called to be distinct from our culture — not superior, arrogant or self-righteous, but different. We're not seeking partial purity in an impure world, but absolute holiness before a holy God.

Sadly, some believers bring compromise into the church. They effectively say, 'I wonder how much sin I can get away with?' But God will not tolerate that kind of attitude. He calls us to purify ourselves from all unrighteousness and walk blamelessly before Him. That doesn't mean that we obey legalistically only because we fear His punishment. It means, rather, that we do His will because we know that He loves us and want to express our love for Him in return.

God is creating a Christlike people. Now we can't change ourselves. The transformation we need is a work that only God can accomplish through the Holy Spirit. That's not to say we become passive. Far from it. We have a clear command to follow: 'Do not conform any longer to the pattern of this world, but be transformed by the renewing of your mind' (Rom. 12:2a). It's

▓ To ponder

The Greek word used in Romans 12 for 'being transformed' is *metamorphomai* from which our English word 'metamorphosis' is derived.

A tadpole undergoes a metamorphosis; it simply eats and gradually limbs sprout and it turns into a frog. Similarly as we feed on God we will be transformed, becoming more and more like Jesus.

▓ To meditate on

Jesus is looking for a holy people. 'Christ loved the church and gave himself up for her to make her holy ... and to present her to himself as a radiant church, without stain or wrinkle or any other blemish, but holy and blameless' (Eph. 5:25b–27).
'But we know that when he appears, we shall be like him, for we shall see him as he is. Everyone who has this hope in him purifies himself, just as he is pure' (1 John 3:2b,3).

our responsibility to resist worldliness and to renew our minds, and we do that by devoting ourselves to spiritual disciplines.

These disciplines don't transform us. But practising the spiritual disciplines positions us to be transformed by God Himself. They are the means of grace that He has provided. As we study, meditate on and obey the Word, we put ourselves in a position to be transformed by the Spirit.

Although Jesus needed no transformation, He still disciplined His life. In obedience to the Spirit, He went into the desert where he fasted, worshipped, prayed and meditated. His reliance on the Spirit, coupled with a practice of the spiritual disciplines, gave Him a decisive victory over the enemy and empowered Him throughout His ministry.

It will be no different for us as we emulate our Lord's lifestyle in private as well as public. As we privately devote ourselves to the spiritual disciplines and depend entirely on the Holy Spirit we will be transformed. And the result? A dynamic company of people who reflect the character of God and perform powerfully in public.

▮ To analyse

Are you still trying to change yourself in your own strength or are you relying on the Holy Spirit to transform you?

Instead of putting your effort into rigid self-control, put your effort into devoting yourself to the spiritual disciplines and developing your relationship with the Holy Spirit.

▮ Food for thought

➢ Meditate on Philippians 2:12,13.

➢ What is our responsibility? What will God do? How does this free us from striving?

➢ What response do you need to make to this?

The Word has power to enlighten our darkness; in our hearts it will bring the light of God, the sense of His love, and the knowledge of His will. The Word can fill us with strength and courage to conquer every enemy, and to do whatever God asks us to do. The Word would cleanse and sanctify; it would work in us faith and obedience; it would become in us the seed of every trait in the likeness of our Lord. Through the Word the Spirit would lead us into all truth, that is, make all that is in the Word true in us, and so prepare our hearts to be the habitation of the Father and the Son ... God's Word has omnipotent power in the heart to work every blessing of which it speaks.
Andrew Murray

❑ STUDY 30

'If my people, who are called by my name, will humble themselves and pray and seek my face and turn from their wicked ways, then will I hear from heaven and will forgive their sin and will heal their land' (2 Chr. 7:14).

Challenge

A few years ago a friend and I attended a conference in Seoul, South Korea. At the beginning of the week, Yonggi Cho took us up Prayer Mountain and said, 'I want you to see this first because you must know that whatever happens during the conference is a direct result of what's going on here.'

Bus after bus pulled in. Many of their occupants were taking a day off, but instead of relaxing, shopping or playing sport they were pouring into a huge auditorium to pray. There were no regrets. They clearly wanted to be there.

I joined them in one of the regular prayer meetings. There were thousands in the room — ordinary believers with an unmistakeable passion for God, crying out to Him, weeping before Him, possessing a fervency that overwhelmed me. I couldn't understand what they were saying, but I longed for the passion that they demonstrated.

Outside were the grottos, empty little huts where individuals could pray. Nothing about these huts would prompt you to declare, 'I'd really love to spend a few days in that.' But people consistently come. Dr Cho said that if

▨ To ask

What is your response when you read about this kind of fervency in prayer?

Do you allow it to challenge you or do you write it off as being unattainable for you?

▨ To meditate on

We must be diligent in prayer.
'Look to the Lord and his strength; seek his face always (1 Chr. 16:11).
'Pray continually' (1 Thess 5:17).
'And pray in the Spirit on all occasions with all kinds of prayers and requests' (Eph. 6:18a).

Christians are struggling with a problem, the leaders assign them three days of prayer and fasting at Prayer Mountain.

I wondered how many of us would be willing to accept that sort of directive. 'Right, no more counselling. This is your prescription: three days of prayer and fasting.' Teachable believers will respond to that because they're not seeking sympathy from people but solutions from God. Above all else they want to know God's answer to their need and they'll do anything — however costly — to discover it.

For the church in Seoul Korea, daily fervent intercession is the norm. When I visited, there were two all-night prayer meetings a week, and both were filled to capacity. I will never forget the Sunday meeting when Dr Cho led the church in prayer. I had never experienced such passion and power.

My time there was a life-changing event. I came home thinking about the verse, 'my house will be called a house of prayer for all nations' (Isa. 56:7b), and it struck me that God is looking not for a few keen individuals, but for a church of people who are seeking Him with all their hearts.

Food for thought

➢ What should we be praying for?

➢ Using a concordance make a list of subjects and people we should pray for, e.g. 'pray for kings and all those in authority' (1 Tim. 2:2a).

➢ Incorporate this list in your daily devotional times.

To consider

Are you part of the prayer life of your church?

Do you regularly attend prayer meetings?

How can you play a part in your church becoming 'a house of prayer'?

God isn't going to ask us how quickly we built but how well.
Charles Simpson

STUDY 31

I press on to take hold of that for which Christ Jesus took hold of me (Phil. 3:12b).

Your Kingdom come!

Jesus said, 'I will build my church' (Matt. 16:18b). When we pray, 'Your Kingdom come, your will be done!' we are asking God to rule in and through the church. But if we try to build our own kingdoms — pursue our priorities — then we hinder God's purposes for our lives. God wants us to be so devoted to His supreme objective that we willingly renounce anything that conflicts with it. That's radical obedience, and it should be the norm.

I know many individuals who have refused to be seduced by our culture and who have sacrificed a great deal for the Kingdom of God. Several of them could have become wealthy, but decided instead to receive a moderate salary and spend more time with their family and working with the church. They aren't trying to seek attention; they simply want to serve.

Such people realise that abundant life is nothing to do with pursuing self-fulfilment through self-gratification. They know that it's about laying down their lives. They are no longer motivated by selfish ambition. Their sole concern is to establish a church that accurately represents Jesus in His character and power, a church that will provoke the world to jealousy.

▩ To choose

Moses, who had been brought up in the Royal Family, chose to despise his wealth and upbringing and to associate himself with the Israelites.

You, too, have a choice to make.

Will you choose not to be drawn into our culture but to lay down your life and to establish a glorious church?

▩ To meditate on

Let's finish well.
'Throw off everything that hinders and the sin that so easily entangles, and let us run with perseverance the race marked out for us. Let us fix our eyes on Jesus, the author and perfecter of our faith, who for the joy set before him endured the cross, scorning its shame ... Consider him who endured such opposition from sinful men, so that you will not grow weary and lose heart' (Heb. 12:1b–3).